Better Homes and Gardens

ENCYCLOPEDIA of COOKING

Volume 5

Delectable Apricot-Coconut Ring rates high with coconut fans. Cake mix bakes in ring mold atop brown sugar-coconut glaze. To serve, spoon glaze over apricots mounded in cake ring.

On the cover: Golden harvest corn is studded with plump, tender kernels. A versatile vegetable, corn appeals to all ages whether served on-the-cob or added to soups or casseroles.

BETTER HOMES AND GARDENS BOOKS
NEW YORK • DES MOINES

Printed in the United States of America.
First Edition. Second Printing, 1971.
Library of Congress Catalog Card Number: 73-129265
SBN 696-02005-X

COCONUT, COCOANUT—The fruit of the coconut palm. It is used as a beverage, as a food, and as a cooking oil.

Often found growing along the sandy seashore, the wide distribution of the coconut palm is due to the sturdy character of its fruit. The coconut, relatively light in weight, has a fibrous husk with a leathery skin that prevents it from becoming waterlogged. When dropped from trees growing along the shore into the sea, the coconuts are carried by tides and currents to distant shores where they germinate readily on sandy beaches. Today, coconut palms are found abundantly in Indonesia and other southeast Asian countries, the Philippines, and tropical America.

The coconut palm matures in about seven years and will produce fruit for 70 to 80 years. When unripe or green, the coconut is filled with a rich, cold milk. This is an important beverage on the tropical islands. The milk is always cold because of the insulation provided by the meat of the fruit. After the milk and meat are removed, the shell of the coconut is often used as a water cup on the islands.

In addition to producing coconuts, the tree is a source of numerous other products, some of which have significant commercial value. The young buds are cut out of the top of the tree and cooked as a vegetable, known as "palm cabbage"; the tree sap is used in making wine, liquor, and vinegar; the trunk provides lumber; the leaves are used for making fans, baskets, and thatched roofs; and the husk of the coconut yields a durable fiber, important in making ropes, cords, and brushes.

Copra (dried coconut meat), the major export product of many of the smaller islands, is pressed to obtain coconut oil. A white, solid substance at room temperature, it is used for cooking and for manufacturing candles, soap, and margarine. Coconut oil is also used in making suntan lotions and other toiletry items.

Nutritional value: One-fourth cup of fresh, shredded coconut provides about 84 calories while dried, shredded coconut has a somewhat higher caloric value. In addition, coconut contains very small amounts of some vitamins and minerals.

How to select: Fresh coconuts are available throughout the year in most markets, but the peak season is from October through December. Select those that are heavy for their size and whose liquid can be heard sloshing around inside when shaken. Avoid coconuts without milk and those whose three soft spots or "eyes" at the top of the shell are wet and moldy.

Coconut is also available in the supermarket shredded, grated, or flaked. Marketed in various sized cans or packages, it may be dry or moist, sweetened or unsweetened. It is also available toasted.

How to store: An uncracked coconut may be stored at room temperature for one to two months. Once it is cracked, it should be refrigerated in a tightly covered container. Freshly grated coconut can be kept three to four days in the refrigerator or stored for many months in the freezer.

Packaged coconut stays fresh on the kitchen shelf in the unopened container for several months. After opening, it must be refrigerated in a tightly covered container to maintain freshness. Like freshly grated coconut, the storage life of packaged coconut is prolonged if frozen.

How to prepare: The husk and shell of the coconut must be removed before the meat can be eaten or prepared for use in baking. First, using a sharp instrument such as an ice pick, pierce the three eyes of the coconut and drain the milk. Then tap all over with a hammer until the shell cracks and falls off or can be pulled off.

Another method for removing the shell of the coconut is to heat the drained coconut in the oven at 350° for 30 minutes. The shell will crack, making it easier to remove; however, it may still be necessary to tap lightly with a hammer to complete the cracking of the shell.

Depending upon how the coconut is used, the brown tissue covering the meat may or may not be removed. For all-white coconut, use a vegetable parer or a sharp knife to remove the brown covering. To shred coconut, cut the peeled meat into small cubes and grate, using an electric blender, a shredder attachment of an electric mixer, or a hand shredder.

How to use: Both the milk and the meat of the coconut can be used as a beverage, as a cooking ingredient, and for eating.

Although milk drained from the ripe coconut can be drunk, it is quite thin and watery. A thicker, and more palatable milk, sometimes used in Latin American and Polynesian cookery, can be made at home by squeezing freshly grated coconut through cheesecloth to extract the milk. Or, the grated coconut can be heated with cow's milk, simmered over low heat until the mixture begins to foam, and then strained. This milk can be chilled and served as a beverage or used in cooking.

Coconut meat is often eaten out-of-hand as a confection or grated for use in baked products. A popular ingredient in candymaking, coconut is also used extensively in salads, pies, cakes, cookies, ice creams, and many fruit desserts. An attractive garnish, coconut is easily minted, tinted, or toasted for use as a dessert topper.

How to tint or toast coconut

Tinted Coconut: Add a few drops of food coloring to grated or shredded coconut in a screw-top jar. Cover and shake vigorously until all the coconut is evenly colored.

Toasted Coconut: Spread a thin layer of grated or shredded coconut in a shallow baking pan. Toast in the oven at 350° till lightly browned, about 6 to 7 minutes. Shake pan or stir often during toasting to insure even toasting of coconut.

Canned coconut chips which have been toasted and salted are convenient for sprinkling over desserts such as puddings, ice creams, or fresh fruit cups. Crisp and crunchy, they are delicious when served on a snack tray or combined with mixed nuts. If desired, coconut chips can be made at home from a fresh coconut by thinly slicing the coconut meat into short strips, using a vegetable parer. Toast the coconut strips in the oven as for grated coconut, except sprinkle lightly with salt.

Apricot-Coconut Ring

1 30-ounce can apricot halves
3 tablespoons butter or margarine
1/3 cup brown sugar
2/3 cup flaked coconut
1 package 1-layer-size white cake mix
2 tablespoons brown sugar
1 tablespoon cornstarch

Drain apricots; reserve syrup. In saucepan heat butter, 3 tablespoons syrup, and 1/3 cup brown sugar till butter melts and sugar dissolves. Pour into greased 5½-cup ring mold. Sprinkle with coconut. Prepare cake mix according to label directions; spoon over coconut. Bake at 350° till cake tests done, about 25 minutes. Cool for 1 minute; invert on serving plate. Remove ring mold. Pile apricots in center.

To prepare glaze, mix 2 tablespoons brown sugar with cornstarch in saucepan. Add remaining apricot syrup. Bring to boiling. Cook, stirring constantly, till thick and clear. Spoon glaze over cake and apricots. Serves 6 to 8.

Toasted Coconut Ice Cream

In saucepan cook one 14½-ounce can evaporated milk and ½ cup sugar till sugar dissolves. Cool; stir in 2 teaspoons vanilla. Pour into 11x 7x1½-inch baking pan. Freeze till firm. Place in a cold bowl, breaking mixture into chunks. Beat smooth with electric or rotary beater. Whip 1 cup whipping cream. Fold whipped cream and 2/3 cup toasted coconut into mixture. Return to pan; cover, and freeze. Serves 8.

Minted Coconut

In screw-top jar combine 1 teaspoon water, 6 drops green food coloring (optional), and 4 drops peppermint extract. Add one 3½-ounce can flaked coconut. Cover; shake till mixed.

A cream pie classic

Sprinkle coconut liberally over meringue → just before Coconut Cream Pie goes into the oven. Coconut toasts while top browns.

Coconut Diamonds

Chewy, brown sugar topping adds richness—

6 tablespoons butter, softened
1/4 cup granulated sugar
1/4 teaspoon salt
1 cup sifted all-purpose flour
. . .
2 eggs
1 teaspoon vanilla
1 cup brown sugar
2 tablespoons all-purpose flour
1/2 teaspoon salt
1 cup flaked coconut
1/2 cup coarsely chopped walnuts

Cream together softened butter, 1/4 cup granulated sugar, and 1/4 teaspoon salt till light and fluffy. Stir in 1 cup flour. Pat mixture into bottom of 9x9x2-inch pan. Bake at 350° till lightly browned, about 15 minutes.

Meanwhile, beat eggs slightly; add vanilla. Gradually add brown sugar, beating just till blended. Stir in 2 tablespoons flour and 1/2 teaspoon salt. Add flaked coconut and chopped walnuts; mix well. Spread mixture over baked layer. Return to oven and bake 20 minutes longer or till wooden pick comes out clean. Cool. Cut in diamonds. Makes 1 1/2 dozen.

Coffee-Coconut Ice Cream Balls

Frozen ice cream balls make a quick dessert—

Vanilla ice cream
1 1/2 teaspoons instant coffee powder
1 1/2 teaspoons water
1 3 1/2-ounce can flaked coconut (1 1/3 cups)
Chocolate sauce

Chill cookie sheet in freezer. Place scoops of ice cream on chilled cookie sheet; freeze.

Meanwhile, in screw-top jar combine instant coffee powder, water, and flaked coconut. Cover; shake till well mixed.

Remove frozen ice cream balls from freezer. Roll in coffee-coconut mixture. Return to freezer. Store frozen ice cream balls in clear plastic bag in freezer till ready to use.

To serve, place ice cream balls in sherbets. Top dessert with chocolate sauce.

Coconut-Oatmeal Cookies

2 cups quick-cooking rolled oats
2/3 cup flaked coconut
. . .
1 cup butter or margarine, softened
1 cup sugar
2 eggs
3 tablespoons milk
1 1/2 teaspoons vanilla
1 1/2 cups sifted all-purpose flour
1/2 teaspoon baking soda
1/2 teaspoon salt
. . .
Sugar
Flaked coconut

In shallow baking pan combine oats and 2/3 cup coconut. Toast in the oven at 350° till lightly browned, about 6 to 7 minutes. Shake pan or stir often to insure even browning.

Cream butter with 1 cup sugar till fluffy. Add eggs, milk, and vanilla; beat well. Sift together flour, baking soda, and salt; add to creamed mixture, blending well. Stir in toasted coconut-oat mixture. Drop from teaspoon, 2 inches apart, on *ungreased* cookie sheet.

Flatten with a tumbler dipped in sugar. Sprinkle tops with untoasted flaked coconut. Bake at 400° for 8 to 10 minutes. Remove at once from pan; cool. Makes 4 dozen.

Puncture "eyes" of coconut with ice pick to drain milk. If a thicker milk is desired, squeeze meat of coconut to extract liquid.

Coconut Cream Pie

¾ cup sugar
⅓ cup all-purpose flour *or*
3 tablespoons cornstarch
2 cups milk
3 slightly beaten egg yolks
2 tablespoons butter or margarine
1 teaspoon vanilla
1 cup flaked or shredded coconut
1 *baked* 9-inch pastry shell, cooled
Meringue
⅓ cup flaked or shredded coconut

Combine sugar, flour, and ¼ teaspoon salt. Gradually stir in milk, mixing well. Cook and stir over medium heat till thickened and bubbly. Cook 2 minutes more. Remove from heat. Stir small amount hot mixture into egg yolks; immediately return to hot mixture. Cook and stir 2 minutes. Remove from heat. Add butter, vanilla, and 1 cup coconut. Pour the mixture into the 9-inch cooled pastry shell.

Spread Meringue atop hot filling, sealing to edge of pastry. Sprinkle Meringue with the ⅓ cup coconut. Bake at 350° till golden brown, about 12 to 15 minutes. Cool.

Meringue: Beat 3 egg whites with ½ teaspoon vanilla and ¼ teaspoon cream of tartar till soft peaks form. Gradually add 6 tablespoons sugar, beating till stiff peaks form and all sugar is dissolved. Spread the meringue atop the pie.

Crisp and lightly browned, coconut chips add crunch and glamour to desserts when sprinkled over fruit, ice cream, or sherbet.

There's no need to frost this Pineapple Crunch Cake; the coconut-brown sugar topping is spread on the cake before baking.

Pineapple Crunch Cake

1 8¾-ounce can crushed pineapple (1 cup)
⅓ cup shortening
½ cup granulated sugar
1 teaspoon vanilla
1 egg
1½ cups sifted all-purpose flour
1½ teaspoons baking powder
¼ teaspoon salt
½ cup flaked coconut
⅓ cup brown sugar
⅓ cup chopped walnuts
3 tablespoons butter or margarine, melted

Drain pineapple *thoroughly*, reserving ½ cup syrup. Thoroughly cream shortening, granulated sugar, and vanilla. Add egg; beat well. Sift together dry ingredients; add to creamed mixture alternately with reserved syrup, beating after each addition. Spread *half* of the batter evenly in greased and floured 8x1½-inch cake pan; spoon pineapple over. Cover with remaining batter. Combine coconut, brown sugar, walnuts, and butter; sprinkle over batter. Bake at 350° till done, about 35 to 40 minutes. Serve warm with ice cream, if desired.

COD—A lean, saltwater fish found in North Atlantic waters. Relatives of the cod are found in North Pacific waters and colder regions of the Southern Hemisphere, but their commercial value is of little significance. Cod is of great economic importance to New England, Newfoundland, Norway, and Iceland.

The average cod weighs about ten pounds and grows to a length of three feet; some, however, weigh over 100 pounds and attain a length of five feet. Although their color varies, they are generally olive green on top with darker spots and white on the underside, and with a conspicuous white lateral line along the side.

The natural habitat of cod is near the bottom of the sea where it preys upon nearly all other fish except sharks.

Much of the cod catch is split, dried, and salted on the vessel immediately after it is caught. It is sold flaked, shredded, pickled, smoked, or unsmoked. Unsalted cod is available in frozen fillets in most inland areas, while fresh cod is most plentiful near the source of supply. Fresh or frozen fillets are cooked in much the same manner as ocean perch or haddock. The liver of cod is used commercially in making cod liver oil. (See also *Fish*.)

Codfish Balls

- **½ pound salt-cod**
- **3 cups diced, peeled, raw potatoes**
- **1 beaten egg**
- **2 tablespoons butter or margarine**
- **Fat for frying**

Soak cod in water several hours or overnight. Drain and dice. Cook potatoes and cod in boiling water till potatoes are tender; drain. Beat with electric mixer. Add egg, butter, and ¼ teaspoon pepper; beat well. Drop by heaping tablespoons (size of golf balls) into deep, hot fat (375°). Fry till golden brown, 2 to 3 minutes; turn once. Drain. Makes 30.

CODDLE—To gently cook food in water just below the boiling point. Eggs in the shell are often cooked in this manner.

COFFEE—1. A beverage made from the ground and roasted seeds of a tall, tropical plant. 2. The seeds, green or roasted which are ground and used to make the beverage.

The bean and the beverage have a history as varied as their uses. The little bean has been banned, blessed, and smuggled. To some people, coffee is simply a leisure-time drink; to others it is a means of economic livelihood. But, whatever, from the time of its discovery, coffee has led the world a merry dance.

According to legend, it all began when a Mediterranean goatherd, Kaldi, tasted the bean of a wild cherry after the fashion of his frisky goats. When he, too, became pepped-up, he reported his find to his local priest who dipped the bean in hot water and drank the unsweetened brew. From then on, the monks drank coffee to help them through long ceremonies.

The church, in fact, has done a great deal to promote the spread of coffee. When Mohammedan priests realized that Turkish villagers were spending the mandatory hour of daily prayer gossiping over a cup of coffee, they declared the brew alcohol, forbidden by the *Koran*, and banned it.

Not to be outdone, Pope Clementine VII accepted that what was bad for the Mohammedans was good for the Christians and promptly blessed the bean into the church, thus popularizing the beverage.

Later, during the Crusades, when the Austrian army was driving the Turkish forces from the Holy Land, an Austrian soldier, Franz George Kolschitzky, was rewarded for his heroics with all the Turkish coffee that was left behind after the expulsion. With this large supply he started a coffee shop in Vienna.

Before long, the idea of coffee shops spread across the European continent. Men would spend afternoons in these coffee emporiums, discussing the politics of the day. In fact, it was in such a shop, Boston's Green Dragon Coffeehouse, that the Boston Tea Party was planned.

The establishment of the coffee break would seem to be a natural extension of the British tea break, but this is not the case. It stemmed from the coffeehouse idea. The officers of the old Mississippi Steamship Line in New Orleans decided in

1930 that the Brazilian tradition of breaking for coffee in the morning and in the afternoon had multiple benefits to the company—psychologically and economically.

Initially, the major supply of coffee was grown in Java. This was until a Franciscan monk, Father Villase, who wished to aid his poor parishioners, smuggled the closely guarded plant out of Java and into Rio de Janeiro where he planted it in the monastery gardens. From this improbable beginning stems the domination of Brazil as a grower and exporter of coffee.

In the early years of colonial America, coffee was purchased green, then roasted at home. Then, in 1790, a New York businessman opened the first coffee-roasting plant. Here the beans were roasted over a slow coal fire and crudely packaged in newspaper for retail sale. Although such commercial roasting was not readily accepted, inventors persisted in the development of better roasting machines.

The first ground and roasted coffee appeared on the New York market in the early 1860s. Methods of packaging improved within the next few years. In 1900, the first vacuum-packed coffee appeared on the market, thereby providing coffee that retained its aromatic qualities.

How coffee is produced: Coffee trees grow best in a well-watered, tropical climate, preferably at a high altitude, and under a constant temperature of 65 to 70 degrees. Because of these conditions, it is not possible to grow coffee in the United States, except for a small amount of Kona coffee grown in Hawaii. The major coffee growing countries are Brazil, El Savador, Columbia, Costa Rica, Guatemala, Arabia, India, Java, and Malaya.

The coffee tree, which doesn't mature for about five years, is shrublike and bears a fruit known as cherries. When ripe, these cherries are red; however, the plant often bears blossoms and green and red cherries at the same time. Consequently, the cherries must be hand-picked.

Each cherry has two coffee beans in its center. Once the beans are removed, the pulp of the cherry is discarded. The first step in production of coffee after cleaning involves the blending of various types of

Use one package of pudding to make two coffee-flavored desserts—Chocolate Almond Cups and Mocha Marshmallow Pudding.

beans. After the correct blend is achieved, the beans are carefully roasted to develop a characteristic flavor and color. During roasting, the bean "pops" and increases to nearly twice its size.

Mechanization has greatly reduced the possibility of damage to the coffee bean that was once of great concern to the roasters. The individual coffee beans are loaded onto large hoppers from which a large number of blends can be made. These blends are computer selected to ensure that the coffee is clean and the blend is roasted at the right temperature—generally at 360° for 15 minutes. Different degrees of roasting produce different flavors of coffee. Names of different roasts include cinnamon, high, New York, Chicago, New Orleans, French, and Italian.

Coffee can be brewed from the whole, roasted bean, but a quicker and more flavorful cup of coffee is prepared from ground beans. Although of no nutritional value, tannins are responsible for much of the characteristic flavor of coffee. Desirable in small amounts, too much tannin results in a bitter-flavored coffee.

Various commercial grinds of coffee are made for use in different types of coffee makers. Home-type coffee grinders are still popular in some homes despite the fact that the grind is generally not as uniform as that ground commercially.

After grinding, the coffee is vacuum-packed to prevent staling, thus insuring maximum retention of the aromatic oils. The sudden, rich aroma and pressure release which accompanies the opening of a vacuum-packed can of coffee is due to carbon dioxide given off by the coffee within the can after it is packed.

Nutritional value: Coffee contains caffein which acts as a mild stimulant to the body. For people who wish to avoid caffein, decaffeinated coffee is available in which most of the caffein has been removed.

A few minerals and a substance which is converted to the B vitamin, niacin, are present in coffee but in very small amounts. A pleasant beverage, coffee, when served with a meal, enhances the enjoyment of other foods rather than contributing important nutrients to the diet.

Types of coffee: Over 100 different kinds of coffee, each with its own flavor, are found throughout the world. Unlike so many other foods, there is no "best" coffee, although each nation has its favorite. Italians and French are more accustomed to a heavy or dark-roast coffee while Americans prefer a medium-roast coffee. Even within the United States, a variation in coffee preferences exists. Along the West Coast, coffee is lightly roasted, is light in color, and has a sharp flavor. Moving eastward, it gets progressively darker. Coffee is darkest around New York, but it is also very dark in the South where it is often blended with chicory. Most brands found on the market today are a blend of several coffees which accounts for numerous flavor variations.

A major boon to the coffee industry was the development of instant coffee. This offers a much easier-to-prepare cup of coffee and, to many people, an equally satisfying drink. To manufacture this product, roasted, ground coffee is brewed with water. The grounds are discarded and the coffee brew is dried. The powder which remains after drying is packaged and sold as instant coffee. A somewhat different procedure is used to make freeze-dried coffee. This coffee brew is first frozen, then the moisture is removed in a vacuum, producing dry, brittle crystals of coffee which dissolve readily in water.

How to select: Personal preference determines whether regular, instant, freeze-dried, or decaffeinated coffee is purchased. If regular coffee is used, however, the grind should be selected on the basis of the method used to prepare the coffee.

Regular grind is best suited for steeped or percolator coffee, drip grind for drip coffee, and fine grind for vacuum coffee. A more recent development is a special grind designed for use in electric percolators. As a rule, it is best to use the finest grind of coffee possible for the particular method of coffee making, as this allows a greater surface area of the coffee to be exposed to the water. Thus, a richer, more full-bodied flavor results in the beverage.

How to store: Exposing ground coffee to the air causes staling which in turn produces a weaker flavored coffee. After opening, coffee retains its freshness best when stored in the refrigerator or freezer in a tightly covered container. To avoid long storage, purchase coffee in amounts which will be used within a short time.

How to use: Coffee is served most often either plain or with cream and/or sugar. Combined with other ingredients, it serves as the basis for many special drinks such as café au lait, café brûlot, and Irish coffee. The roasted coffee bean is also used as an ingredient in a wide variety of desserts. Added either in dry form, as instant coffee powder, or in liquid form, the strong flavor of coffee blends very well with chocolate, butterscotch and a multitude of other spices. (See also *Beverage*.)

How to make coffee

Start with a clean coffee maker. Clean well after each use to remove oils that collect.
Use fresh, cold water for making coffee.
Measure accurately. Allow 2 level measuring tablespoons coffee (or 1 coffee measure) for each ¾ cup standard measuring cup water. Proportions may vary with individual taste, brand of coffee, and coffee maker.
For best results, use the full capacity of coffee maker and never boil coffee.
Accurate timing is important. Find the best timing, then stick to it.

Automatic Coffee: Follow the directions given by manufacturer.

Percolator Coffee: Measure cold water into percolator. Measure coffee into basket. Cover; place over heat. Bring to boiling; reduce heat. Perk *gently* 6 to 8 minutes. Remove basket; keep hot over *very low heat.*

Vacuum Coffee: Measure cold water into lower bowl; place over heat. Insert filter and correct measure of finely ground coffee in upper bowl. When water boils, insert upper bowl into lower bowl. When water rises to top, stir mixture. Reduce heat. After 2 or 3 minutes, remove from heat. Let coffee return to lower bowl before removing upper bowl.

Drip Coffee: Bring cold water to boiling. Measure coffee into coffee basket; pour boiling water in top water container. Let drip through coffee. Remove basket and water container and stir briskly.

Instant Coffee: For each cup place 1 rounded teaspoon instant coffee powder and ¾ cup boiling water into coffeepot. Heat over *low* heat 5 minutes. Or, prepare in cup.

To prepare coffee over an open fire, measure water plus a little extra to make up for that which boils away. Bring to a hard, rolling boil. Add 1 heaping tablespoon coffee for each cup water. Boil 1 minute, then set off coals but close enough to fire to keep hot.

To prepare iced coffee, brew coffee using *half* the amount of water for the usual amount of coffee. Pour hot coffee into ice-filled tumblers. *Or,* dissolve two rounded teaspoons instant coffee powder in one-half glass cold water; add ice and stir well.

Capped with whipped cream and spicy gingersnap crumbs, Coffee-Chiffon Torte is the perfect ending for an elegant meal.

Chocolate Coffee

1 cup water
2 1-ounce squares unsweetened chocolate
1/4 cup sugar
2 tablespoons instant coffee powder
Dash salt
. . .
3 cups milk
Whipped cream

In saucepan combine water, chocolate, sugar, instant coffee powder, and salt; stir over low heat just till chocolate melts.

Gradually add milk to chocolate mixture, stirring constantly. When piping hot, *but not boiling*, remove mixture from heat and beat with rotary beater till frothy.

To serve, pour chocolate coffee into cups or mugs. Spoon a dollop of whipped cream atop each serving. Makes 6 servings.

Swedish Egg Coffee

In small bowl combine 1 slightly beaten egg (reserve shell) and 2/3 cup coffee. (If stronger coffee is desired, use 1 cup coffee.) Add 1/2 cup cold water; blend well. Stir in crumbled egg shell. Add to 8 cups boiling water.

Heat and stir over high heat till foam disappears, about 4 minutes. Remove from heat; cover. Let settle for about 7 to 10 minutes. Serve clear coffee off top, or strain through fine mesh strainer. Makes 10 servings.

Café Aruba

3 cups hot double-strength coffee
1/4 cup orange peel cut in very thin strips
1 orange, peeled and sliced
1 tablespoon sugar
1 teaspoon aromatic bitters
1/2 cup whipping cream

Measure hot coffee into glass pot. Add orange peel and slices. Let mixture steep over low heat for 15 minutes. Add sugar and bitters. *Do not boil.* Strain; pour into warmed glasses or mugs. Whip cream; sweeten to taste, if desired. Spoon atop coffee. Serves 4 or 5.

Cool Coffee Eggnog

4 cups milk
2 beaten egg yolks
1/4 cup sugar
2 tablespoons instant coffee powder
1 teaspoon vanilla
1/4 teaspoon salt
. . .
2 egg whites
3 tablespoons sugar

In medium saucepan stir milk into beaten egg yolks. Add 1/4 cup sugar, instant coffee powder, vanilla, and salt. Cook over medium heat, stirring constantly, till mixture coats a metal spoon. Remove from heat and chill.

Just before serving, beat egg whites till foamy. Gradually add 3 tablespoons sugar, beating to soft peaks. Add to chilled coffee mixture; mix thoroughly. Makes 6 to 8 servings.

Spiced Iced Coffee

2 tablespoons sugar
2 tablespoons instant coffee powder
1/4 teaspoon ground cinnamon
1 1/2 cups milk
2 cups cola beverage, chilled

Combine sugar, instant coffee powder, and ground cinnamon. Stir in milk. Blend in blender or with rotary beater till well mixed. Add cola; stir gently just till combined. Pour into ice-filled tumblers. Makes 6 servings.

Brazilian Float

In saucepan heat together one 1-ounce square unsweetened chocolate and 2 tablespoons sugar till chocolate melts and sugar dissolves. Remove from heat. Stir in 1/2 cup strong hot coffee. Add 2 cups hot milk; mix well. Chill. Scoop 1 pint vanilla ice cream into 4 glasses; add chocolate mixture and stir. Serves 4.

Almond-Coffee Tortoni

A dessert to have on hand for unexpected guests—

1/2 cup whipping cream
2 tablespoons sugar
1/2 teaspoon vanilla
2 drops almond extract

• • •

1 egg white
2 tablespoons sugar

• • •

2 tablespoons finely chopped almonds, toasted
2 tablespoons coconut, toasted
1/2 teaspoon instant coffee powder

In small mixing bowl whip cream with 2 tablespoons sugar, vanilla, and almond extract. Beat egg white to soft peaks. Gradually add 2 tablespoons sugar; beat to stiff peaks.

Mix toasted almonds and coconut. Fold beaten egg white, almond-coconut mixture, and instant coffee powder into whipped cream. Spoon dessert mixture into 4 paper bake cups in muffin pan. Sprinkle remaining nut mixture over all. Freeze till firm. Makes 4 servings.

Coffee Chiffon Torte

Spicy gingersnaps add crunch—

2 envelopes (2 tablespoons) unflavored gelatin
1/2 cup sugar
1/2 teaspoon salt
4 teaspoons instant coffee powder
3 cups milk
3 beaten egg yolks
3 egg whites
1 teaspoon vanilla
1/4 teaspoon cream of tartar
4 gingersnaps, crushed (1/3 cup)
Whipped cream

In saucepan mix gelatin, sugar, salt, and coffee powder. Combine milk and beaten egg yolks. Add to gelatin mixture. Cook and stir till gelatin and sugar dissolve and mixture thickens slightly. Chill till partially set.

Beat together egg whites, vanilla, and cream of tartar till soft peaks form. Fold in gelatin mixture. Chill till mixture mounds.

Spoon mixture into 6 1/2-cup mold. Chill till firm. Unmold onto serving dish. At serving time, sprinkle mold with *half* the gingersnap crumbs. Spoon whipped cream atop mold; garnish with remaining crumbs. Makes 8 servings.

Mocha-Marshmallow Pudding and Chocolate-Almond Cups

1 6 3/4-ounce package *instant* chocolate pudding mix
2 tablespoons sugar
1 tablespoon instant coffee powder
1/2 cup miniature marshmallows
2 tablespoons chopped almonds, toasted

Prepare pudding according to package directions, adding sugar and coffee powder to dry mix. Divide mixture in half. *Mocha-Marshmallow Pudding:* To *half* the pudding mixture, add marshmallows. Pile in 4 sherbets. Makes 4 servings. *Chocolate-Almond Cups:* To remaining *half* of the pudding mixture, add almonds. Spoon into 4 foil or paper bake cups in muffin pans. Freeze. Remove desserts from muffin pan; wrap, and return to freezer. Serves 4.

Kona Coffee Torte

A delectable dessert with an orange filling—

Cake:
- **1½ tablespoons instant coffee powder**
- **6 egg yolks**
- **2 cups granulated sugar**
- **2 cups sifted all-purpose flour**
- **3 teaspoons baking powder**
- **1 teaspoon vanilla**
- **1 cup ground walnuts**
- **6 stiff-beaten egg whites**

Orange Filling:
- **1 cup butter, softened**
- **2 cups sifted confectioners' sugar**
- **2 teaspoons unsweetened cocoa powder**
- **½ teaspoon instant coffee powder**
- **2 tablespoons orange juice**

Mocha Frosting:
- **2 cups sifted confectioners' sugar**
- **2 teaspoons unsweetened cocoa powder**
- **½ teaspoon instant coffee powder**
- **3 tablespoons butter, melted**
- **½ teaspoon vanilla**

Cake: Dissolve 1½ tablespoons coffee powder in 1 cup cold water. Beat egg yolks till light and fluffy. Gradually add granulated sugar, beating till thick. Sift together flour, baking powder, and ¼ teaspoon salt. Add to yolks alternately with dissolved coffee; beat well after each addition. Add 1 teaspoon vanilla and nuts. Fold in stiff-beaten egg whites.

Bake in 3 paper-lined 9x1½-inch round cake pans at 325° for 30 minutes. Cool 10 minutes. Remove from pans; cool. Fill cake with Orange Filling; frost top with Mocha Frosting.

Orange Filling: Cream 1 cup softened butter with 2 cups sifted confectioners' sugar. Beat in 2 teaspoons unsweetened cocoa powder, ½ teaspoon instant coffee powder, 2 tablespoons cold water, and orange juice.

Mocha Frosting: Mix 2 cups sifted confectioners' sugar, 2 teaspoons unsweetened cocoa powder, and ½ teaspoon instant coffee powder. Add 2 tablespoons cold water; 3 tablespoons butter, melted; and ½ teaspoon vanilla. Beat till frosting is of spreading consistency.

Ice Cream Sundae Mold

- **¼ cup flaked coconut, toasted**
- **1½ teaspoons brandy flavoring**
- **1 quart vanilla ice cream, softened**
- **¼ cup slivered almonds, toasted**
- **1 quart coffee ice cream, softened**
- **Fudgy Chocolate Sauce**

Stir coconut and brandy flavoring into vanilla ice cream; turn into 6½-cup mold. Freeze till firm. Stir almonds into coffee ice cream; spoon into mold atop frozen vanilla layer. Freeze firm, about 5 hours. Unmold. Drizzle with Fudgy Chocolate Sauce; sprinkle with additional toasted almonds, if desired. Pass remaining sauce. Makes 10 to 12 servings.

Fudgy Chocolate Sauce: In saucepan combine one 6-ounce package semisweet chocolate pieces and ⅔ cup light corn syrup; stir over low heat till chocolate melts. Cool. Blend in one 6-ounce can evaporated milk (⅔ cup).

Coffee Chiffon Pie

- **⅓ cup sugar**
- **1 envelope (1 tablespoon) unflavored gelatin**
- **1 tablespoon instant coffee powder**
- **¼ teaspoon ground nutmeg**
- **3 slightly beaten egg yolks**
- **1 14½-ounce can evaporated milk**
- **½ teaspoon vanilla**
- **3 egg whites**
- **⅓ cup sugar**
- **1 *baked* 9-inch pastry shell (See *Pastry*)**
- **½ cup whipping cream**

In saucepan combine first 4 ingredients and dash salt. Combine egg yolks and evaporated milk; stir into gelatin mixture. Cook and stir till gelatin dissolves and mixture thickens slightly. Stir in vanilla. Chill till partially set, stirring often. Beat smooth.

Beat egg whites to soft peaks; gradually add ⅓ cup sugar, beating to stiff peaks. Fold in gelatin mixture. Pile in baked pastry shell. Chill till firm. Whip cream. Top pie with whipped cream and chocolate curls, if desired.

A dessert to top all desserts—Ice Cream Sundae Mold. Fudgy Chocolate Sauce flows generously down layers of coffee and vanilla ice cream studded with toasted almonds and coconut.

Coffee Angel Pie

2 egg whites
½ teaspoon vanilla
¼ teaspoon salt
¼ teaspoon cream of tartar
½ cup sugar
½ cup finely chopped pecans
1 pint coffee ice cream
1 pint vanilla ice cream

• • •

Caramel-Raisin Sauce

Beat together egg whites, vanilla, salt, and cream of tartar till soft peaks form. Gradually beat in sugar till very stiff peaks form and sugar is dissolved. Fold in pecans. Spread in well-buttered 9-inch pie plate, building up sides to form a shell. Bake at 275° for 1 hour. Turn off heat; let dry in oven, with door closed, for 1 hour. Remove from oven; cool.

Pile scoops of coffee and vanilla ice cream into cooled shell; freeze till firm. Let pie stand 20 minutes at room temperature before serving. Cut in wedges to serve.

Serve with *Caramel-Raisin Sauce:* In small saucepan melt 3 tablespoons butter or margarine; stir in 1 cup brown sugar, 1 6-ounce can evaporated milk (⅔ cup), and dash salt. Cook over medium-low heat, stirring constantly, till sugar dissolves and mixture boils. Remove from heat; stir in ½ cup golden raisins and 1 teaspoon vanilla. Cool sauce slightly. Spoon over pie. Makes 1⅓ cups sauce.

COFFEE CAKE, COFFEE BREAD—Rich, sweet cake or bread served at breakfast, brunch, or the mid-morning coffee break, rather than as a dessert.

There are two types of coffee cake. One type resembles bread because it's made with yeast; the other is more like cake because of the leavening effect on the batter by the baking powder or baking soda. Both types are enriched with eggs or egg yolks and sweetened with sugar. In addition, fruits, nuts, and spices, such as cinnamon and nutmeg, are used to flavor the dough, filling, or topping.

Coffee cakes are shaped in many different designs. The dough can be arranged in pinwheels, sunburst circles, braids, and Christmas trees. The shape can also be formed by baking in loaf, oblong, square, round, and tube or bundt pans.

Toppings make a coffee cake more attractive and appealing. Confectioners' icing is frequently drizzled over the warm bread. Nuts, candied fruit, raisins, and streusel topping can be sprinkled over the top for variety in flavor, appearance, and texture.

Coffee cake is usually served warm from the oven in the morning. Its addition to a mid-morning coffee break or coffee klatch completes the affair whether the gathering is formal or informal. A hot bread is a must for brunch menus, and coffee cakes are favorites with both the hostess and guests. At breakfast, these sweet, hot breads make the simplest menu seem glamorous. A menu of bacon or Canadian-style bacon, eggs, cups of piping-hot coffee, and a fruit with the coffee cake will make a weekend breakfast special, dress up a family breakfast, or impress company.

How to prepare with convenience products: Both the bread- and cake-type coffee cakes can be made using convenience products. Biscuit and hot roll mix form the foundation with fruit, nuts, and spices added for flavoring. Other mixes, for instance muffin mixes, already have much of the flavoring and only require minor adaptation. Refrigerated biscuits and rolls are probably the quickest and easiest convenience products to use. They can be dipped in melted butter, sugar and spices, and nuts, or filled with a favorite fruit mixture.

Miniature Brunch Loaf

2 tablespoons chopped pecans
3 tablespoons brown sugar
1 cup packaged biscuit mix
1/4 teaspoon ground cinnamon
1/8 teaspoon ground mace
• • •
3 tablespoons milk
1 egg
2 tablespoons butter, melted
1/4 teaspoon vanilla

Mix pecans with *2 tablespoons* brown sugar; set aside. Combine the biscuit mix, remaining brown sugar, cinnamon, and mace. Combine milk, egg, *1 tablespoon* of the melted butter, and vanilla. Make a well in the center of dry ingredients; add liquid all at once.

Stir with fork till blended. Spoon *half* of the biscuit mixture into greased 5½x3x2¼-inch loaf pan; brush with *some* of the remaining butter and sprinkle with *half* of the pecan mixture. Repeat with remainder of the biscuit mixture, butter, and pecans. Bake at 350° for 25 to 30 minutes. Serve warm.

Pear-Berry Coffee Cake

3 fresh pears, peeled and cored
1 teaspoon lemon juice
1/2 cup brown sugar
1/2 cup sifted all-purpose flour
1/4 teaspoon ground nutmeg
1/4 cup butter or margarine
1 13½-ounce package blueberry muffin mix

Slice pears lengthwise into eighths. Sprinkle with lemon juice. Mix sugar, flour, and nutmeg together; cut in butter. Prepare muffin mix according to package directions. Turn into greased 9x9x2-inch pan. Top with pears. Spoon crumbly mixture over. Bake at 400° about 35 minutes. Makes 9 servings.

Visions of sugarplums

Studded with almonds and cherries and → drizzled with rich syrup, Sugarplum Ring makes a welcome gift or highlights a brunch.

Prune-Nut Braid

1 13¾-ounce package hot roll mix
2 tablespoons butter or margarine, melted and cooled
1 teaspoon grated orange peel
¾ cup canned prune filling
¼ cup chopped pecans
Confectioners' Icing

Prepare hot roll mix according to package directions. Add butter or margarine and orange peel; mix well. Cover; let rise in warm place till doubled, about 1 hour. On lightly floured surface, knead dough about 1 minute. Roll dough to a 12-inch square. Cut into 3 strips.

Spread ¼ cup prune filling down center of each strip. Sprinkle evenly with nuts. Pinch dough up around filling to form 3 ropes. Place on greased baking sheet and braid dough; pinch ends together. Cover and let rise till almost doubled, about 40 minutes. Bake at 375° till done about 25 minutes. Glaze while warm with confectioners' icing and decorate with red sugar and pecans, if desired. Serve warm.

Confectioners' Icing: Combine 1 cup confectioners' sugar, 1 to 1½ tablespoons milk, and ¼ teaspoon vanilla. Mix till smooth.

Serve a gala breakfast on even the busiest mornings by using refrigerated rolls to make a ring of Quick Apple Pinwheels.

Quick Apple Pinwheels

1 8-ounce package refrigerated crescent rolls (8 rolls)
1 medium apple, cored, peeled, and chopped (about 1 cup)
¼ cup raisins
2 tablespoons granulated sugar
½ teaspoon grated lemon peel
Dash ground nutmeg
Milk
1 tablespoon brown sugar

Separate crescent rolls. On greased baking sheet, arrange triangles, bases overlapping, in complete circle. (Center of circle should be *open*, with points toward *outside*.) Combine apple, raisins, granulated sugar, lemon peel, and nutmeg. Spoon apple filling mixture over bases of triangles. Fold points over filling, tucking points under bases of triangles at center circle. Brush with a little milk; sprinkle with brown sugar. Bake at 350° till golden brown, about 25 minutes.

How to prepare using the quick method: Coffee cakes made by the quick method use baking powder or baking soda for leavening and are not kneaded. Resembling cake more than bread in texture, they may have a more open grain and uneven surface than coffee cakes made with yeast. This method, however, takes much less time and work. The coffee cake can be mixed quickly and baked in time for breakfast or served to unexpected guests.

Coffee Cake

Combine ¼ cup salad oil, 1 beaten egg, and ½ cup milk. Sift together 1½ cups sifted all-purpose flour, ¾ cup granulated sugar, 2 teaspoons baking powder, and ½ teaspoon salt. Add dry ingredients to milk mixture; mix well. Pour into greased 9x9x2-inch pan.

Combine ¼ cup brown sugar, 1 tablespoon all-purpose flour, 1 teaspoon ground cinnamon, 1 tablespoon melted butter or margarine, and ½ cup broken nuts. Sprinkle over batter in pan.

Bake coffee cake at 375° till done, about 25 minutes. Serve cake warm.

Orange-Date Coffee Cake

2 cups sifted all-purpose flour
½ cup granulated sugar
3 teaspoons baking powder
½ teaspoon salt
1 slightly beaten egg
½ cup milk
½ cup salad oil
½ cup snipped dates
2 teaspoons grated orange peel
½ cup orange juice
2 tablespoons butter or margarine, softened
½ cup brown sugar
1 teaspoon ground cinnamon
½ cup chopped walnuts

In large bowl, sift together flour, granulated sugar, baking powder, and salt. Combine egg, milk, and salad oil; add all at once to dry ingredients. Stir just till well blended. Combine dates, orange peel, and orange juice; stir into batter just till blended. Spread batter evenly in greased 11x7x1½-inch baking pan. Combine butter, brown sugar, cinnamon, and nuts. Sprinkle over batter. Bake at 375° for 25 to 30 minutes. Serve warm.

End the search for something different to serve at breakfast or at coffee by baking the lightly spiced Orange-Date Coffee Cake.

Toasted Coconut Coffee Cake

3 cups sifted all-purpose flour
1 cup sugar
4 teaspoons baking powder
1 teaspoon salt
1 3½-ounce can flaked coconut, toasted (1⅓ cups)
2 teaspoons shredded orange peel
1 slightly beaten egg
1½ cups milk
2 tablespoons salad oil
1 teaspoon vanilla

In mixing bowl, sift together flour, sugar, baking powder, and salt. Stir in toasted coconut and orange peel. Combine egg, milk, oil, and vanilla; add to dry ingredients all at once, stirring just till combined. Turn batter into greased 9x5x3-inch loaf pan. Bake at 350° till done, 60 to 70 minutes. Remove from pan. Cool on rack. Makes 1 loaf.

Apricot-Almond Coffee Cake

¾ cup dried apricots, snipped
Milk
¼ cup shortening
¾ cup granulated sugar
1 egg
1½ cups sifted all-purpose flour
2 teaspoons baking powder
¾ teaspoon salt
½ teaspoon ground cinnamon
½ cup brown sugar
⅓ cup all-purpose flour
4 tablespoons butter or margarine
⅓ cup chopped almonds

In saucepan, combine apricots and 1 cup water; simmer, uncovered, 15 minutes. Cool. Drain, adding enough milk to liquid to make ½ cup. Cream together shortening and granulated sugar. Add egg and beat well. Sift together the 1½ cups flour, baking powder, salt, and cinnamon. Add to creamed mixture alternately with the milk mixture, beginning and ending with dry ingredients; stir in apricots. Turn into greased 9x1½-inch layer cake pan or 9x9x2-inch baking pan. Combine brown sugar and the ⅓ cup flour; cut in butter or margarine till crumbly; add almonds. Sprinkle over batter. Bake at 350° for 40 to 45 minutes. Serve warm.

Cowboy Coffee Cake

2½ cups sifted all-purpose flour
2 cups brown sugar
½ teaspoon salt
⅔ cup shortening

• • •

2 teaspoons baking powder
½ teaspoon baking soda
½ teaspoon ground cinnamon
½ teaspoon ground nutmeg
1 cup sour milk
2 beaten eggs

Mix flour, sugar, salt, and shortening till crumbly; reserve ½ cup. To remaining crumbs, add baking powder, baking soda, cinnamon, and nutmeg; mix well. Add sour milk and eggs; mix well. Pour into 2 greased and floured 8x1½-inch round pans; top with reserved ½ cup crumbs. Bake at 375° for 25 to 30 minutes. Serve warm. Makes 2 cakes.

Banana Coffee Bread

½ cup shortening
1 cup sugar
2 eggs
¾ cup mashed ripe banana

• • •

1¼ cups sifted all-purpose flour
¾ teaspoon baking soda
½ teaspoon salt

Cream shortening and sugar till fluffy. Add eggs, one at a time, beating well after each. Stir in banana. Sift together flour, baking soda, and salt; add to banana mixture. Mix well. Pour into greased 9x9x2-inch pan. Bake at 350° for 30 to 35 minutes.

How to prepare using yeast method: Coffee cakes made with yeast resemble bread but are sweeter and richer. This method takes more time to prepare than the quick method and usually requires kneading. However, the end product, like homemade bread, is well worth all the effort required.

Coffee cakes can be baked and frozen for later use. If the recipe yields two cakes, serve one and freeze the other. Or, make two recipes while all the ingredients, mixing bowls, and utensils are out. Wrap the baked coffee cakes in foil and freeze. Those made with yeast can be stored for as long as six to eight months.

When ready to use, thaw the bread in its wrapper at room temperature allowing about three hours. The bread can also be heated in the foil wrapper at 325° for 15 to 20 minutes to thaw and reheat it at the same time. (See also *Bread.*)

Sugarplum Ring

1 package active dry yeast
3¾ to 4 cups sifted all-purpose flour
¾ cup milk
⅓ cup sugar
⅓ cup shortening
1 teaspoon salt
2 beaten eggs

• • •

¼ cup butter or margarine, melted
¾ cup sugar
1 teaspoon ground cinnamon
½ cup whole blanched almonds
½ cup candied whole red cherries
⅓ cup dark corn syrup

In large mixer bowl, combine yeast and *2 cups* flour. Heat milk, the ⅓ cup sugar, shortening, and salt just till warm, stirring occasionally to melt shortening. Add to dry mixture in mixing bowl; add eggs. Beat at low speed with electric mixer for ½ minute, scraping sides of bowl constantly. Beat 3 minutes at high speed. Stir in by hand enough of the remaining flour to make a soft dough. Mix thoroughly and place in a greased bowl, turning once to grease surface. Cover and let rise till double, about 2 hours. Punch down and let rest 10 minutes.

Divide dough into 4 parts. Cut each part into 10 pieces and shape into balls. Dip balls in the melted butter, then in the ¾ cup sugar blended with the cinnamon. Arrange ⅓ of the balls in well-greased 10-inch tube pan. Sprinkle with some of the almonds and cherries. Repeat with two more layers. Mix corn syrup with butter left from dipping balls; drizzle over top.

Cover and let rise in warm place till double, about 1 hour. Bake at 350° for 35 minutes. Cool 5 minutes; invert pan and remove ring.

Chocolate Chip Coffee Ring

In large mixer bowl, combine 1 package active dry yeast and 1¼ cups sifted all-purpose flour. Heat together ½ cup milk, ¼ cup butter or margarine, 3 tablespoons sugar, and ½ teaspoon salt just till warm, stirring occasionally to melt butter. Add to dry mixture in bowl; add 1 egg. Beat at low speed of electric mixer for ½ minute, scraping sides of bowl constantly. Beat 3 minutes at high speed. By hand, stir in ½ cup sifted all-purpose flour. Add ½ cup semisweet chocolate pieces; mix well. Turn into well-greased 4½-cup ring mold. Cover; let rise till double, 45 minutes to 1 hour.

Bake at 400° for 12 to 15 minutes. Remove from pan immediately; drizzle with confectioners' sugar icing while warm.

English Tea Ring

1 package active dry yeast
2½ to 2¾ cups sifted all-purpose flour
¾ cup milk
¼ cup sugar
¼ cup shortening
1 beaten egg
½ teaspoon vanilla
¼ cup sugar
1 teaspoon ground cinnamon
½ cup chopped walnuts
½ cup chopped mixed candied fruits and peels

In large mixer bowl, combine yeast and 1½ *cups* flour. Heat milk, ¼ cup sugar, shortening, and 1 teaspoon salt just till warm, stirring occasionally to melt shortening. Add to dry mixture; add beaten egg and vanilla. Beat at low speed with electric mixer for ½ minute, scraping sides of bowl constantly. Beat 3 minutes at high speed. By hand, stir in enough of the remaining flour to make a soft dough. Knead lightly on floured surface. Place in a greased bowl; turn once to grease surface. Cover; let rise till double in bulk, 1½ to 2 hours.

Roll to 13x9-inch rectangle, about ¼ inch thick. Brush with melted butter; spread evenly with Fruit Filling. Roll starting from long side, like jelly roll. Seal edge. Shape in a ring on greased baking sheet. With scissors, snip almost to center at 1-inch intervals. Pull sections apart and twist slightly. Let rise till double, 35 to 45 minutes. Bake in a 375° oven for about 20 to 25 minutes.

Fruit Filling: Mix ¼ cup sugar, ground cinnamon, walnuts, and candied fruits.

Swedish Holiday Braid

1 package active dry yeast
5½ to 6 cups sifted all-purpose flour
1½ teaspoons ground cardamom
¼ teaspoon ground mace
1¼ cups milk
½ cup sugar
½ cup butter, margarine, or shortening, softened
2 beaten eggs
1 cup dark or light raisins
Sugar Glaze

In large mixer bowl combine yeast, 2¾ *cups* flour, cardamom, and mace. Heat milk, sugar, butter, and 2 teaspoons salt just till warm, stirring to melt butter. Add to dry mixture; add eggs. Beat at low speed with electric mixer for ½ minute, scraping sides of bowl constantly. Beat 3 minutes at high speed. Add raisins. By hand, stir in enough of the remaining flour to make a soft dough.

Turn out on a lightly floured surface and knead till smooth and elastic, about 8 to 10 minutes. Place in a lightly greased bowl, turning once to grease surface. Cover and let rise in warm place till double in bulk, about 1½ hours. Punch down.

Divide and round the dough into 2 balls, one for each braid. Cover and let rest for 10 minutes. For each braid: divide one ball in thirds. Shape into strands 15 inches long, tapering the ends. Line up the strands 1 inch apart on a lightly greased baking sheet. Braid loosely without stretching the dough, beginning in the middle, and working toward either end. Seal ends well. Repeat with second half.

Cover and let rise in a warm place till double, about 45 minutes. Bake at 350° for about 25 to 30 minutes. While warm, spread with Sugar Glaze. Makes 2 braided loaves.

Sugar Glaze: To 1 cup sifted confectioners' sugar, add 2 tablespoons hot water and 1 teaspoon butter or margarine. Mix till well blended. Drizzle over warm braids.

Shaping ropes of dough in a circle forms the Sunburst Coffee Cake design. Raisins, cherries, and citron fill the inside while confectioners' icing and cherry halves garnish the top.

To shape coffee cake: Divide dough into 12 pieces; roll each to form 8-inch ropes. Place 6 ropes, twisted in a U-shape, around 4-inch circle in center of baking sheet.

Form the remaining 6 ropes in O-shapes; join seamed ends at center of circle, allowing rounded end to overlap the first layer of U-shapes at a point in between the petals.

Sugarplum Loaves

In large mixer bowl, combine 2 packages active dry yeast and 2½ cups sifted all-purpose flour. Heat 1¼ cups milk, ½ cup sugar, ¼ cup shortening, and 1½ teaspoons salt just till warm, stirring occasionally to melt shortening. Add to dry mixture in mixer bowl; add 1 teaspoon grated lemon peel and 2 beaten eggs. Beat at low speed with electric mixer for ½ minute, scraping sides of bowl constantly. Beat 3 minutes at high speed. Add 1½ cups chopped, mixed candied fruits and peels. By hand, stir in 2¼ to 2¾ cups sifted all-purpose flour or enough flour to make a soft dough.

Knead on lightly floured surface till smooth and elastic, 6 to 8 minutes. Place in lightly greased bowl, turning once to grease surface. Cover; let rise in warm place till double in bulk, 1½ to 2 hours. Punch dough down. Divide dough in half; round each into a ball. Cover and let rest 10 minutes.

Pat balls of dough into 2 round loaves. Place on greased baking sheet; pat tops to flatten slightly. Cover and let rise till double, about 1½ hours. Bake at 350° about 30 minutes. (Cover tops with foil after about 25 minutes to prevent over-browning.) Cool. While still slightly warm, frost with Confectioners' Icing, and decorate with chopped nuts or nut halves and candied fruits. Makes 2 loaves.

Sunburst Coffee Cake

2 packages active dry yeast
2¾ to 3 cups sifted all-purpose flour
¾ cup milk
¼ cup sugar
¼ cup shortening
1 egg
½ cup raisins
¼ cup candied cherries, cut up
2 tablespoons chopped candied citron

In large mixing bowl, combine yeast and 1½ *cups* flour. Heat milk, sugar, shortening, and 1 teaspoon salt just till warm, stirring occasionally to melt butter. Add to dry mixture in bowl; add egg. Beat at low speed with electric mixer for ½ minute, scraping sides of bowl constantly. Beat 3 minutes at high speed.

Add raisins, cherries, and citron. By hand, stir in enough of the remaining flour to make a soft dough. Turn out on lightly floured surface; knead till smooth, 5 to 8 minutes. Place in a greased bowl, turning dough once. Cover and let rise till double, 1½ hours.

Punch down; turn out on a lightly floured surface. Cover and let rest 10 minutes. Divide dough into 12 equal pieces. With hands roll each piece into a rope 8 inches long and ¾ inch thick. On lightly greased baking sheet, arrange 6 pieces in a U-shape around a 4-inch circle with ends toward the center. Make the remaining 6 pieces into oval shapes and arrange over the U-shapes, with ends joining in the center. Let rise till double, about 1 hour. Bake at 350° till done, about 25 minutes. Drizzle with Confectioners' Icing and garnish with candied cherries, if desired.

Golden Crown Coffee Bread

2 packages active dry yeast
7 tablespoons butter or margarine
¾ cup sugar
3 eggs
½ cup milk, scalded and cooled
3¾ cups sifted all-purpose flour
¾ cup light raisins
2 teaspoons grated lemon peel
3 tablespoons fine dry bread crumbs
Blanched whole almonds
Confectioners' sugar

Soften yeast in ½ cup *warm* water. In mixing bowl, cream *6 tablespoons* butter and granulated sugar until light; add eggs, one at a time, beating after each. Add softened yeast, milk, flour, and 1½ teaspoons salt. Beat at medium speed on mixer till smooth, about 2 minutes. Stir in raisins and lemon peel. Cover and let rise till double, 1½ to 2 hours.

Meanwhile, melt remaining butter. Prepare a 3-quart bundt pan or Turk's Head mold: brush liberally with melted butter and sprinkle with bread crumbs, coating well. Arrange almonds in a design on bottom of mold. Stir down batter; spoon carefully into mold. Let rise till almost double, about 1 hour. Bake at 350° till done, 25 to 30 minutes. Let stand 5 minutes; remove from mold. Cool and lightly sift confectioners' sugar over top.

COFFEE CREAM—Another name for 18 percent light cream. (See also *Light Cream.*)

COFFEE GRINDER *or* MILL—Equipment, hand or electrically driven, that grinds whole, roasted coffee beans. Home-sized grinders help achieve a freshly brewed coffee flavor. (See also *Coffee.*)

COFFEE MAKER—Any unit that is designed primarily to brew the hot beverage, coffee. (See also *Coffee.*)

COGNAC *(kōn' yak)*—A brandy produced around Cognac, a town in the province of Charente, in western France. The name "cognac" is protected by laws which specifically define the region and processing methods to be used when making it. No other brandies can be labeled "cognac."

Distillation of cognac began in the 1600s as a result of high taxes placed on the bulk exports of wines. The distilled wines were stronger, less bulky, brought higher prices, and provided a very palatable natural brandy superior to other liquors. Over the years, cognac has maintained this outstanding reputation.

The high quality of cognac is due to the lime soil of the district where the grapes are grown as well as to the careful distillation and aging processes the grapes undergo. St. Émilion grapes are the primary variety used, but Folle-Blanche and Colombard are also employed.

When fermentation is complete, the wine is distilled twice in traditional copperpot stills. These successive distillations produce a raw product with an alcoholic content of up to 135 proof.

The colorless liquid is then poured into barrels made of local or Limousin oak where a unique aging process takes place. No other variety of oak can produce the same characteristics. During aging, the brandy absorbs tannic acid from the barrels; this causes the color to darken and the flavor to change. Oxidation taking place in the porous wood develops the characteristic bouquet and flavor.

Because cognac is a blend, there are no vintage years. Each distiller develops his personal flavor style which he achieves, year after year, through careful blending procedures. After several months or years of maturation, the blended brandy is bottled. Once bottled, cognac, like all distilled liquors, does not change either in color or in flavor. (See also *Brandy.*)

Gourmet Salad

In skillet brown ½ pound chicken livers in 2 tablespoons butter or margarine. Add ½ teaspoon salt; ¼ teaspoon dried thyme leaves, crushed; and dash pepper. Remove livers.

In bowl blend ¼ cup mayonnaise or salad dressing, 1 tablespoon instant minced onion, 1 tablespoon water, and 1 tablespoon cognac (brandy). Chop livers coarsely. Add liver, ½ cup minced celery, and 2 teaspoons snipped parsley to mayonnaise mixture. Mix well; chill.

Arrange lettuce leaves on 4 chilled salad plates. Place 1 thick tomato slice on each plate; salt lightly. Spoon liver mixture onto each tomato slice. Makes 4 servings.

The colander with its functional design is ideal for tasks that involve draining foods such as vegetables and pastas.

Cold cuts identification

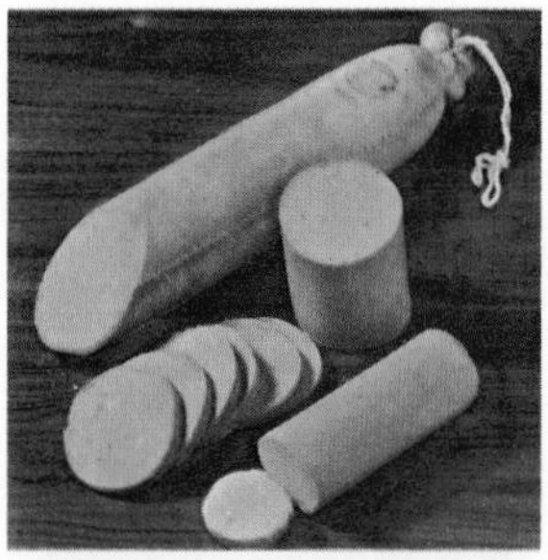

Left: Braunschweiger is a cooked, smoked, liver sausage that is named after the German town where it was first developed.

Right: Luncheon meats include many combinations of meats and seasonings that are cooked or baked into loaves before slicing.

Left: Cooked lamb and pork tongues are arranged lengthwise in the center of a blood sausage roll made of diced or finely ground cooked meat, beef blood, and spices.

Right: Peppered loaf combines coarsely ground cooked beef and pork with cracked peppercorns. The peppercorns give delightful old-fashioned flavor and texture.

Left: Edible portions of pork heads are cooked, chopped, and mixed with a spiced gelatin base for headcheese. Modern formulas may include pork tongue or heart.

Right: Minced roll is a cooked, smoked cold cut made with finely ground beef and pork sausage. Caraway seed adds distinctive flavor to this roll—ideal for sandwiches or just plain in-between-meal nibbling.

COLA—A carbonated beverage made with a sugar syrup and flavored with an extract of kola nuts, the bitter fruits of a tropical tree. (See *Carbonated Beverage, Kola Nut* for additional information.)

COLANDER ***(kul' uhn duhr)***—A large round, perforated bowl, usually with two handles on opposite sides, made of metal or plastic. It is useful for draining liquid from foods as when rinsing noodles or spaghetti. The word "colander" is derived from a Latin word that means "to strain."

COLCANNON ***(kuhl kan' uhn)***—An Irish vegetable dish made by mashing potatoes, kale or other greens, and scallions. The mixture is combined with butter, milk, salt, pepper, and parsley.

COLD CUT—The general term for meat that is ready to eat and available fresh, canned, or packaged. Cold cuts include cooked sausages such as braunschweiger or salami, canned luncheon meats, sliced luncheon loaves, boiled ham, cured or smoked meats, and prepared meat loaves available from the delicatessen counter.

Cold cuts can be the beginning of quick-to-fix sandwiches, salads, and cold meat platters. Cold cuts and sliced cheeses, accompanied by plenty of raw vegetable relishes and an assortment of sliced dark and white breads, make a hearty self-service supper for family or buffet entertaining. Another popular use is to arrange cold cut slices or rolls around a platter, alternating them, and then to heap potato salad in the center of the platter.

Cold cuts identification

Left: Olive loaf, a mild pork and beef combination, is colored and flavored with stuffed olives and sweet red peppers.

Right: Thuringer is a semidry summer sausage which may be either lightly or heavily smoked. It has a tangy lactic acid flavor.

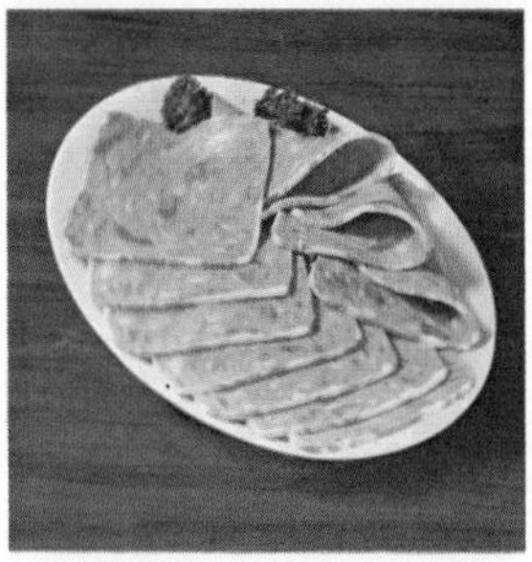

Left: A delicate sweet flavor pervades in another versatile cold cut, honey loaf. As its name indicates, the lean pork or pork-beef mixture is seasoned with honey.

Right: Dry salamis are made of cured pork and beef, highly seasoned with garlic and other spices, and moistened with red wine or grape juice. The mixtures are stuffed in natural casings and air-dried.

Left: Jellied beef loaf has been developed for the roast beef sandwich fans. Cooked beef is shredded or chopped, mixed with gelatin, and molded into a round or rectangular loaf that is ready to slice for use.

Right: Pepperoni, named for its pepper spicing, is coarsely chopped meat, seasoned, cured, and then air-dried.

Left: Chopped ham is a popular cold cut with the hamlike flavor and color of cured pork. The ground, chopped, or cubed meat is formed into a firm loaf.

Right: Genoa salami (right), an Italian specialty, is identified by a light garlic flavor. Cervelatwurst (left) is a mildly seasoned summer sausage of Germany.

Left: Summer sausage was first made in northern Europe as a method of preserving meat for the summer. Today, it is a family name for smoked, semidry sausages.

Right: Frizzes, Italian dry sausages, may be purchased with sweet spices (blue string) or hot spices (red string, being sliced). Frizzes carry an abundance of flavor so slice each piece thinly for most satisfactory results.

COLESLAW—A salad made of shredded, crisp cabbage with well-seasoned mayonnaise or vinegar-based dressing. There are many color and flavor variations of coleslaw with added ingredients such as fruits, vegetables, and seasonings. The name is derived from the Dutch *kool* meaning cabbage and *sla* meaning salad. (See *Cabbage, Salad* for additional information.)

Coleslaw

Shred 3 cups cabbage extra fine using chef's knife or grater. To avoid last-minute fuss toss cabbage with ice cubes; hold in refrigerator 1 hour. Remove ice; drain. If desired, add 1/4 cup chopped green pepper or minced onion, *or* 1 cup grated carrots and 1/2 cup raisins.

Toss with one of these slaw dressings:

- Mix 2 to 3 tablespoons sugar, 3 tablespoons vinegar, 2 tablespoons salad oil, and 1 teaspoon salt; stir till sugar dissolves.
- Combine 1/3 cup mayonnaise or salad dressing, 1 tablespoon vinegar, 2 teaspoons sugar, 1/2 teaspoon salt, and 1/2 teaspoon celery seed; stir till sugar dissolves.
- In small bowl blend together 1/2 cup mayonnaise or salad dressing, 2 tablespoons vinegar, and 1 teaspoon prepared mustard.

Caraway Skillet Slaw

Cabbage in a tasty hot dressing can serve as a salad and vegetable—

4 slices bacon
1/4 cup vinegar
2 tablespoons sliced green onion
1 tablespoon brown sugar
1 teaspoon salt

• • •

4 cups shredded cabbage (about 1/2 medium head)
1 teaspoon caraway seed

In medium skillet cook bacon till crisp. Remove bacon; drain and crumble. Measure 1/4 cup bacon drippings; return to skillet. Add vinegar, onion, brown sugar, and salt; heat through. Add cabbage and caraway seed to skillet; toss mixture lightly. Top with crumbled bacon. If desired, garnish with cherry tomatoes. Serves 6.

Spring Garden Toss

4 cups shredded cabbage
1/2 cup chopped celery
1/4 cup chopped green pepper
1/4 cup shredded carrot
1/4 cup sliced radishes
1 tablespoon chopped onion
1/2 cup dairy sour cream
2 tablespoons tarragon vinegar
1 tablespoon sugar
1/2 teaspoon salt

Combine cabbage, celery, green pepper, carrot, radishes, and onion; chill. Combine remaining ingredients; chill thoroughly. Just before serving toss sour cream mixture lightly with vegetable mixture. Makes 8 servings.

Kidney Bean Coleslaw

3 cups shredded cabbage
1 8-ounce can kidney beans, chilled and drained
1/4 cup sweet pickle relish
1/4 cup thinly sliced green onion
1/4 cup mayonnaise or salad dressing
3 tablespoons chili sauce
1/4 teaspoon celery seed

Combine cabbage, kidney beans, pickle relish, and green onion; chill. Blend together mayonnaise, chili sauce, celery seed, and dash salt; toss with cabbage mixture. Makes 10 servings.

Beet and Cabbage Slaw

1/2 16-ounce jar pickled beets
4 cups shredded cabbage
2 tablespoons chopped green pepper
1/2 cup mayonnaise or salad dressing

Drain pickled beets, reserving 1 1/2 tablespoons liquid; chop drained beets. Combine beets, shredded cabbage, and chopped green pepper; chill thoroughly. At serving time, prepare dressing by blending mayonnaise and reserved beet liquid; toss beet dressing lightly with cabbage mixture. Makes 8 servings.

Luncheon meat slices ruffle the coleslaw combination for blue cheese enthusiasts in Blue Cheese Slaw. Paprika-ladened hard-cooked egg slices create additional garnishing glamour.

Blue Cheese Slaw

6 cups shredded cabbage
2 tablespoons chopped canned pimiento
2 tablespoons chopped green onion tops
½ cup dairy sour cream
2 tablespoons mayonnaise
1 tablespoon lemon juice
½ teaspoon sugar
Dash salt
1 4-ounce package blue cheese, crumbled (1 cup)

Combine cabbage, pimiento, and onion tops; chill thoroughly. Mix together remaining ingredients; chill. Pour over cabbage and toss lightly. If desired, garnish bowl of coleslaw with slices of hard-cooked egg and folded luncheon meat ruffles. Makes 4 to 6 servings.

COLLAGEN—A protein substance of meat muscle and end-bone connective tissue.

Collagen in meats is softened by moisture and heat. The moisture may come from natural meat juices or added liquids, as when pot roast is cooked. During the cooking period, collagen is converted to gelatin, thereby producing a more tender, chewable cut of meat. (See also *Meat*.)

COLLARD—A dark green, leafy vegetable closely related to kale. The broad, tall collard leaves do not grow in a head as do other varieties of the cabbage family.

Because collard plants can withstand high heat and humidity, they have been grown in southern areas of the United States for generations. Traditionally, the greens are boiled with salt pork or fatback, but collard leaves can also be simmered, covered, in their own juices.

Fresh collards, when available in the grocery store, should be selected by appearance—fresh and crisp, clean and free of insect injury. Yellow or wilted leaves indicate poor quality. To retain freshness after purchase, keep crushed ice in the package of collards and refrigerate. Frozen collards are also available.

A serving of this cooked leafy vegetable is low in calories, high in vitamin A, and, if not overcooked, a good source of vitamin C. (See *Afro-American Cookery, Cabbage, Greens* for additional information.)

COLLINS—A tall, iced beverage of lemon or lime juice, carbonated water, and usually gin. Rum, brandy, vodka, or whiskey may be substituted for the gin.

COLLOP—A term sometimes used to describe a small piece or slice of meat.

COLOR KEEPER—A granular preparation of ascorbic acid crystals, sugar, and an inert filler designed to keep peeled or cut fruits such as apples, bananas, peaches, and pears from darkening upon exposure to air. The dry color keeper is usually diluted with water for use.

COMB HONEY—Honey that is sold in the beeswax comb. It is often packaged as a cut portion in a wooden box. A piece of comb honey also may be bottled with strained honey. (See also *Honey.*)

COMBINE—To put two or more foods together so they may be blended.

The act of combining can occur at many stages of cooking. Raisins are combined with a cooked sauce to heat them.

In salad preparation, the salad and dressing ingredients are combined separately. Before serving, they are tossed together.

When making a mix-in-one-bowl main dish, the ingredients are combined right in the baking dish—saves unnecessary washing.

COMFIT—A confection consisting of a solid center (such as a piece of fruit, a seed, or a nut) that is coated with sugar.

COMICE PEAR—An exceptionally sweet, juicy, and aromatic winter pear. The Comice pear has a fine, buttery texture and a winelike flavor. This medium- to large-sized pear has a thicker neck than most other varieties, and its pale green to yellow skin is usually blushed with red. Most sources agree that the Comice is the most delicious dessert pear grown; it is often used as the standard by which other pears are judged. Its full name is Doyenne du Comice which means "best in the show."

The Comice was originally cultivated by French and Belgian monks between 1730 and 1850 and reached America in the mid-1800s. This pear gets its name from the Comice Horticole at Angers, France, where it was extensively cultivated.

This pear is too delicate to be cooked, but it's perfect for fruit salads and fresh eating. In recent years, this pear has become increasingly favored for fruit gift boxes. The finest quality Comice pears are available between October and March.

The primary growing area for Comice pears in the United States is the Pacific Coast states of Washington, Oregon, and California. (See also *Pear*.)

COMINO—The Spanish name for the herb cumin. (See also *Cumin*.)

COMPOTE—Fresh, dried, or canned fruits gently cooked in syrup to preserve their shape. A compote may consist of one fruit or a combination of several fruits and may be served hot or cold as a dessert or main dish accompaniment. Compotes may be flavored with spices, wines, and/or liqueurs. In recent years, the definition of compote has expanded to include any fruits marinated in fruit juice or wine.

Delightful anytime dessert

A dollop of sour cream crowns the luscious blend of cherries, raspberries, and strawberries in sparkling Ruby Fruit Compote.

The compote's simple ingredients and preparation invite the cook to experiment with different fruit combinations. Fruits that complement each other's color, shape, texture, and flavor can be combined for a delicious dessert that belies its simplicity. (See also *Dessert.*)

Winter Fruit Compote

A delicious hot dessert for winter evenings—

3 firm-ripe pears, quartered and cored
3 baking apples, quartered and cored
2 oranges, peeled and chunked
1/4 cup raisins
3/4 cup brown sugar
1/2 cup water

Place pears, apples, oranges, and raisins in 2-quart casserole. In small bowl combine brown sugar and water; pour over fruits. Cover and bake at 350° till tender, about 1 hour. Serve warm or cool. Makes 6 servings.

Hot Curried Fruit Compote

1 16-ounce can pear halves, drained
1 16-ounce can peach halves, drained
1 16-ounce can apricot halves, drained
1 13 1/2-ounce can pineapple chunks, drained
2 tablespoons butter or margarine
1/4 cup brown sugar
1 to 1 1/2 teaspoons curry powder
1 17-ounce can pitted dark sweet cherries, drained

Cut pear and peach halves in half. Place pears, peaches, apricots, and pineapple chunks in a 2-quart casserole. In small saucepan melt the butter or margarine; blend in brown sugar and curry powder. Spoon over fruit in casserole. Bake at 325° for 15 minutes.

Add cherries and mix in carefully. Return to oven and bake 15 minutes more. Serve warm, as a meat accompaniment. Serves 8 to 10.

Ruby Fruit Compote

A great brunch starter all year round. During the winter, use frozen strawberries—

1 20-ounce can frozen pitted tart red cherries, thawed
1 10-ounce package frozen raspberries, thawed
1 1/2 tablespoons cornstarch
1 tablespoon lemon juice
1 pint whole fresh strawberries, rinsed and hulled
Dairy sour cream

Drain frozen cherries and raspberries, reserving syrup. Add enough water to syrup to measure 2 1/2 cups. In small saucepan blend cornstarch, dash salt, and reserved syrup. Cook and stir till thickened and clear. Add lemon juice. Stir in cherries, raspberries, and strawberries. If desired, add sugar to taste.

Chill thoroughly. Spoon into sherbets. Top each serving with a generous dollop of dairy sour cream. Makes 8 servings.

Cherry-Berry Compote

1 17-ounce can pitted dark sweet cherries
1 10-ounce package frozen raspberries
2 tablespoons dry sherry

Pour undrained cherries over frozen raspberries; add sherry. Let stand about 1 hour (berries should have some ice crystals remaining). Spoon into 4 to 6 sherbets.

Chilled Breakfast Compote

2 large grapefruit, peeled and sectioned
1 13 1/2-ounce can frozen pineapple chunks, thawed
1/2 cup cranberry juice cocktail
2 or 3 dashes ground cardamom

Combine grapefruit, pineapple chunks, and their juices with cranberry juice cocktail and cardamom. Cover and chill 4 to 6 hours or overnight. Makes about 4 servings.

CONCENTRATE—Term applied to foods or ingredients marketed in undiluted form. This term is used most frequently in association with frozen fruit juice concentrates from which beverages can be made by the addition of water.

CONCH ***(kongk)***—A saltwater shellfish with a spiral shell. (See also *Shellfish.*)

CONDENSED MILK—Sweetened fresh milk that has been thickened by evaporation of a portion of its water content. (See also *Sweetened Condensed Milk.*)

CONDIMENT—Anything used at the table to add flavor to food. The primary purpose of a condiment is to stimulate the taste buds and saliva secretion, thus, greatly increasing the desire for food.

Some of the principal condiments are salt, pepper, butter, vinegar, sugar, mustard, pickles, and catsup. Some foods, such as onions and garlic, are so stimulating to the taste buds and saliva secretion that they serve the double purpose of a delicious food and also a condiment.

Condiments are eaten in such small quantities that their nutritional contribution is minimal, and, except for salt, these substances are not essential to the normal functioning of the body. People, however, have become so accustomed to the flavor imparted by condiments that many foods seem bland and almost inedible without one or more of them.

CONEY—Name sometimes applied to a frankfurter in a long bun. A Coney Island is a coney topped with a spicy, tomato-meat sauce. (See also *Sandwich.*)

Coney Islands

½ pound ground beef
¼ cup water
¼ cup chopped onion
1 clove garlic, minced
1 8-ounce can tomato sauce
½ teaspoon chili powder
½ teaspoon salt
10 frankfurters
10 frankfurter buns

For sauce, brown ground beef slowly but thoroughly in a skillet, breaking with fork till fine. Mix in water, chopped onion, minced garlic, tomato sauce, chili powder, and salt. Simmer, uncovered, for 10 minutes.

Meanwhile, cover frankfurters with cold water; bring to boiling. Simmer 5 minutes. Place franks in heated frankfurter buns; top with prepared mustard and chopped onion, if desired. Spoon hot sauce atop. Serves 10.

CONFECTION—A name given to a candy or sweetmeat. (See also *Candy.*)

CONFECTIONERS' SUGAR—A finely powdered sugar used in icing and candies. This type of sugar is often labeled XXXX. Confectioners' sugar contains about three percent cornstarch to prevent caking.

In any emergency when running slightly short of confectioners' sugar, granulated sugar, pulverized in a blender, can be used to make up the difference. This pulverized sugar is not as fine as confectioners' sugar, however, so it should not be substituted for large quantities of confectioners' sugar. (See also *Sugar.*)

Confectioners' Icing

Add light cream to 2 cups sifted confectioners' sugar for spreading consistency. Add dash salt and 1 teaspoon vanilla.

Caramel-Cream Cheese Frosting

7 vanilla caramels
1 3-ounce package cream cheese, softened
2½ cups sifted confectioners' sugar
⅛ teaspoon salt

Combine caramels and 1 tablespoon hot water in a 2-cup glass measuring cup or small heat-proof glass dish. Place dish in small saucepan of gently boiling water. Heat and stir till caramels melt and sauce is smooth. Cool.

Beat together cream cheese and sugar. Add cooled caramel sauce and salt; mix well. Frosts a 1-layer cake or 18 cupcakes.

Chocolate Crinkle Cookies

1 cup butter or margarine
1⅓ cups sifted confectioners' sugar
2 tablespoons water
1 teaspoon vanilla
2 4-ounce bars sweet cooking chocolate, grated (2 cups)
2 cups sifted all-purpose flour
½ cup finely chopped walnuts

In mixing bowl cream butter or margarine and confectioners' sugar till light and fluffy. Beat in water and vanilla. Add chocolate, flour, and dash salt; mix well. Stir in nuts. Shape into 1-inch balls; place on *ungreased* baking sheet. Bake at 325° till done, about 25 minutes. Cool. Sprinkle with sifted confectioners' sugar, if desired. Makes 6 dozen.

Saucepan Taffy Bars

½ cup shortening
⅓ cup light molasses
¾ cup brown sugar
1 egg
1¼ cups sifted all-purpose flour
½ teaspoon salt
¼ teaspoon baking soda
⅓ cup chopped walnuts
• • •
1½ tablespoons butter or margarine
⅛ teaspoon grated lemon peel
1 to 1¼ cups sifted confectioners' sugar
1 tablespoon lemon juice
¼ teaspoon vanilla

In saucepan heat together shortening and molasses till boiling. Remove from heat; stir in brown sugar. In mixer bowl beat egg; add molasses mixture. Beat till light and fluffy. Sift together flour, salt, and baking soda; stir into molasses mixture. Stir in nuts. Spread in greased 9x9x2-inch baking pan. Bake at 350° till done, about 20 to 25 minutes.

Frost with Lemon Butter Frosting: Cream butter or margarine with grated lemon peel. Gradually blend in ½ *cup* sifted confectioners' sugar. Beat in lemon juice and vanilla. Gradually blend in enough of remaining confectioners' sugar till of spreading consistency.

Add a touch of the tropics to toast or rolls with Peach Conserve. The double fruit conserve can also be a sundae topping.

CONSERVE—A jamlike spread made of several fruits cooked together with sugar. Raisins and nuts are sometimes ingredients.

Plum Conserve

2 pounds Italian plums
1 cup seedless raisins
1 medium orange
3 cups sugar
• • •
½ cup coarsely chopped walnuts

Pit plums. Grind plums, raisins, and orange (with peel). Place fruits in a large saucepan or kettle. Add sugar; bring to boiling. Cook till mixture is thick, about 10 minutes.

Stir in coarsely chopped walnuts. Pour hot conserve into hot, scalded jars. Seal at once. Makes six ½-pint jars.

Peach Conserve

In large saucepan combine 2 pounds fully ripe peaches, scalded, peeled, and mashed (3 cups mashed), and one 6-ounce can frozen orange juice concentrate, thawed; stir in 5 cups sugar. Bring mixture to a *full rolling boil; boil hard 1 minute,* stirring constantly. Remove from heat; immediately stir in one 6-ounce bottle liquid fruit pectin and one 3½-ounce can flaked coconut. Skim off foam with metal spoon. Stir and skim for 7 minutes. Ladle into hot, scalded jars; seal. Makes seven ½-pints.

The double fruit flavor of conserve makes it different from most jams and jellies. Other fruit combinations that make delicious conserve include apples and peaches, apricots and pineapple, and rhubarb and pineapple. (See also *Jelly*.)

CONSOMMÉ ***(kon' suh mā')*** – A clear, rich soup made by boiling down meat or poultry broth until its volume is reduced by about half. The meat or poultry broth used to make consommé should not be heavily seasoned because the boiling down process intensifies the seasonings.

Further reduction of the water content of consommé will result in a product that will gel without added gelatin when chilled. Canned consommé usually contains added gelatin. (See also *Soup*.)

Jellied Consommé

Chill canned condensed consommé (with gelatin added) in refrigerator 3 hours (or 1 hour in freezer). Spoon into chilled sherbets. Garnish with lemon and parsley. *Or*, serve in half a honeydew melon with lime slices.

For a light lunch or refreshing first course, serve Jellied Consommé, topped with sour cream, or Consommé Cooler. Accompany these chilly soups with a variety of crisp crackers.

Consommé Cooler

2 $10\frac{1}{2}$-ounce cans condensed beef consommé
1 cup water
$\frac{1}{4}$ cup finely chopped celery
2 tablespoons finely chopped green onions and tops
1 teaspoon Worcestershire sauce
Few drops bottled hot pepper sauce

Combine ingredients. Chill thoroughly, at least 3 hours, stirring a few times. Float a few unpeeled cucumber slices, if desired. (To flute edges of cucumber slices, run tines of fork down cucumber.) Makes 6 to 8 servings.

Mexican Surprises

2 tablespoons chopped onion
1 clove garlic, crushed
1 tablespoon salad oil
1 $10\frac{1}{2}$-ounce can condensed beef consommé
$\frac{1}{4}$ cup chili sauce
1 beaten egg
$\frac{1}{2}$ cup milk
$1\frac{1}{2}$ cups soft bread crumbs (about 2 slices)
1 teaspoon salt
$1\frac{1}{2}$ pounds ground beef
3 hard-cooked eggs
$\frac{1}{4}$ cup all-purpose flour
$\frac{1}{3}$ cup chopped almonds (optional)

In skillet cook onion and garlic in salad oil till tender. Reserve $\frac{1}{2}$ cup consommé. Add remaining consommé to skillet with chili sauce.

In mixing bowl combine beaten egg, milk, bread crumbs, and salt. Add ground beef; mix well. Cut each of the hard-cooked eggs into 6 wedges. Divide meat mixture into 18 portions. Wet hands; form one portion of meat around each egg wedge. Place meatballs in skillet with consommé mixture. Bring to boiling; reduce heat and simmer, covered, 20 minutes, turning once. Remove meatballs; reserve sauce.

Blend together all-purpose flour and reserved consommé. Stir into reserved sauce in skillet; cook and stir till thickened and bubbly. Pour over meatballs. Sprinkle with chopped almonds, if desired. Makes 6 servings.

Lamb Roll-Ups

12 large romaine leaves
1 slightly beaten egg yolk
$\frac{1}{2}$ cup milk
$\frac{1}{3}$ cup uncooked packaged precooked rice
$\frac{1}{2}$ cup chopped onion
$\frac{3}{4}$ teaspoon salt
Dash pepper
1 pound ground lamb
$\frac{1}{2}$ cup canned condensed beef consommé
1 egg
1 egg white
$1\frac{1}{2}$ tablespoons lemon juice

Soften romaine leaves by dipping leaves in very hot water, then crushing the rib with thumb. Mix together the egg yolk, milk, uncooked rice, onion, salt, and pepper. Add ground lamb and mix thoroughly.

Shape mixture into twelve 3-inch long rolls, using about $\frac{1}{4}$ cup meat mixture for each. Place each roll lengthwise on a softened romaine leaf. Fold sides up over meat so they overlap and tuck in ends; secure with wooden picks. Place rolls in a skillet and pour consommé over. Cover; simmer 30 minutes. Pour off cooking liquid and strain; reserve for sauce.

For Lemon Sauce, beat whole egg with egg white till thick. Slowly beat in lemon juice and reserved cooking liquid. In saucepan stir over low heat till mixture thickens slightly.

Place Lamb Roll-Ups on warm serving platter. Remove wooden picks. Spoon some sauce over rolls and pass remainder. Serves 4 to 6.

CONVENIENCE FOOD—Food and food products that are ready for use as soon as you remove them from their package or container. (See also *Quick Cookery.*)

CONVERTED RICE—Rice that has been parboiled before milling. Converted rice retains more vitamins and minerals than polished rice but takes slightly longer to cook. (See also *Rice.*)

COOKERY—The art of preparing food. Cookery encompasses the combining, seasoning, garnishing, and serving of food that is a pleasure to eat, not just a necessity.

COOKIE

Easy cookies for family munching plus tasty filled and frosted teatime delicacies.

Cookies are small, sweet, flat, or slightly raised cakes. The name comes to us from the Dutch word *koekje,* a diminutive form of *kock* which means cake. Cookies are little cakes made from the same basic ingredients used in cakes, but formed by different methods into assorted attractive shapes. It is said that the first cookies were really tiny test cakes baked to make sure that the oven temperature and the consistency and flavor of the cake batter were just right for baking.

The first type of cookie was used by pagans in northern Europe. Small pieces of dough were imprinted with animal shapes which had been carved in wooden blocks or molds. These baked tokens were used in pagan holiday celebrations. From these crude beginnings came the beautiful molded and pressed cookies such as springerle and spritz, which are Christmas specialties from this part of the world.

Today, cookies are made in most countries, many cookies having a distinctive national character. The cookies of France are dainty and fancy. Those of Spain are thin and spicy. In the Scandinavian countries, cookies are rich, buttery, and specially shaped. Among the choicest being *krumkaker,* baked on a special iron. German cookies may be thin and dainty or large and hearty with plenty of fruits and nuts. The cookies of England, called biscuits, generally are thin, wafer tea biscuits and are not as sweet as those from most countries. Italians also prefer cookies less sweet and frequently use anise as a flavoring.

Because the founding fathers in the New World came from so many national backgrounds, it is natural that the cookies baked by new settlers of successive generations would reflect their homelands. It wasn't long, however, before the new environment and some ingenious uses of local ingredients produced new kinds of cookies.

Early cook books and famous hostesses of the day may have insisted that cookies be made with butter, but the frontier housewife had only lard, suet, or even bear fat to use as shortening. She improvised by flavoring her cookies with spices and sweetening them with honey or molasses. Her family happily munched the results of her efforts so that keeping the cookie crock well filled was as difficult for her as it is for the modern homemaker.

Over the years America has contributed much to the international cookie jar. New England cooks provided snickerdoodles, tangle breeches, and other home-style goodies whose remarkable names were seemingly bestowed just because they were fun to repeat. More recently, brownies and sliced refrigerator cookies came into being as did cookies made with semisweet chocolate pieces. The latter were unique because the chocolate pieces stayed whole during baking. Today, the homemaker may also choose to do her baking from a wide assortment of mixes and ready-to-bake frozen or refrigerated cookies and doughs.

Cookies are favorite sweets with which to end a meal or to nibble in between meals. They come in all shapes, sizes, and flavor combinations, some with nuts and some without. Their food value is primarily to provide calories for energy. The num-

Keep the cookies coming

← Bake Mincemeat Stars, Maple Nut Chews, Cocoa Drops, Oatmeal Chip Cookies, Paul Bunyan Sugar Cookies, Caramel Chews, and Brownies. (See *Brownie* for recipe.)

ber of calories depends upon the size of the cookie and the amount of shortening, sugar, frosting, and candies, fruits, or nuts used in making or decorating them.

Although related to cakes by virtue of common ingredients, the many kinds of cookies are as different from each other as they are from a luscious layer cake. Baking is not even a common characteristic because there are cookies which never enter an oven and some, like *fattigmand,* are cooked by frying in deep fat.

Cookie basics

Shortening is an important ingredient in cookie baking. Butter or margarine are popular for flavor, but certain cookies are made best with a vegetable shortening, oil, or even cream cheese. Various techniques are used for incorporating the shortening. It may be creamed with the sugar, melted with chocolate, or cut into the dry ingredients with a pastry blender.

To a certain degree, the proportion of flour to liquid determines whether the final cookie will be crisp when baked or have a chewy or cakelike texture. The liquid might be milk, sour cream, fruit juice, or one of the flavorings such as vanilla, almond extract, or brandy. Of course, other factors in crispness are the thickness of the dough when it goes into the oven plus baking time and temperature.

Sweetness in cookies is a matter of personal taste. Granulated sugar, confectioners' sugar, brown sugar, honey, and molasses have been used successfully by good cooks in making cookies for centuries. The white sugars are preferred when a light color or the delicate flavor of some special ingredient is to be emphasized. The sweeteners with a dark color and distinctive flavor of their own are excellent in butterscotch bars or spicy mixtures.

The cookies themselves may be as plain or fancy as the cookie baker wishes. Bar cookies are quick to mix and bake. To serve them, simply cut in squares and transfer to a plate. Big, thick, rolled sugar cookies are just the thing for after school with a glass of milk, but the same dough rolled thinner and cut into fancy shapes, is ready to frost and decorate for a party occasion.

In addition, each homemaker has a favorite collection of cookie recipes for special occasions or for rounding out the variety of shapes and flavors offered at a tea or at an open house.

Decorating cookies is as simple as a light dusting of confectioners' sugar or as involved as ornamental frosting piped from a pastry tube. Tinted coconut, whole or chopped nuts, and candied fruits join brightly colored sugars and small candies as toppers for iced or frosted cookies.

How to store

In many households cookies disappear almost as quickly as they are baked; thus, storage is no problem. Nevertheless, there are times when baking ahead is the order of the day and proper storage is essential to maintain the freshness of the cookies.

In the cookie jar: Store *soft cookies* in a container with a tight-fitting lid so that the cookies stay moist. A metal canister or a pottery jar with a snug cover are good choices. Bars and squares should be kept in the metal pan in which they were baked and covered tightly with a lid or foil. If cookies do begin to dry out, a few slices of apple or orange in the cookie jar help mellow and moisten the cookies. Remove the fruit after one or two days.

Store *crisp cookies* in a container with a loose-fitting cover. Thus, soft and crisp cookies should never be stored together. If crisp cookies do lose some of their snap, they can be freshened by heating them briefly in the oven before serving.

In the freezer: Most cookies, baked or unbaked, may be frozen.

Frozen dough stays fresh for up to six months. Pack the dough in a freezer container or form stiff dough into a roll and wrap securely in foil. When thawed the dough will be ready to slice and bake.

Sometimes cookie dough is formed into balls before baking. There is no reason this step can't be done before the dough goes into the freezer. Shape the balls and spread them on a baking sheet and quick-freeze an hour or until firm. Gather up the balls into a plastic bag and return to the freezer.

When it's time to bake the cookies, as many balls as desired can be baked at one time and the remainder left in the plastic bag in the freezer.

Baked cookies can be stored in the freezer for up to 12 months in plastic bags or foil. The fragile varieties are safer from possible breakage when packed in freezer containers with tight-fitting lids. When ready to serve the baked cookies, thaw them in the freezer wrappings.

Special storage: Students and servicemen welcome a package of home-baked goodies. The kinds of cookies as well as the packing used influence safe delivery.

Cookie mailing tips

Choose soft cookies for mailing. They are better travelers than those that are crisp and breakable. Fruit-filled drops, bar cookies, or brownies pack easily and stand up well in transit. Avoid frostings and fillings that become sticky at room temperature.

A strong cardboard box or metal container is essential. Line the box with waxed paper or foil and put a cushion of crumpled newspaper, waxed paper, or plastic wrap on the bottom. Popcorn or puffed cereal should be avoided as packing materials because they sometimes attract various insects.

Wrap cookies individually or in pairs back to back using clear plastic wrap. Pack the wrapped cookies snugly in rows. Cover each layer with a cushion of crushed waxed paper or paper towels. Bar cookies baked in foil pans can be sent without removing from the pan. Be sure to allow enough space at the top of the packing box or container for a repeat of the insulation layer at the bottom.

Pack metal container, if used, into a heavy cardboard carton using crushed newspaper or confetti to hold securely. Tape box shut and tie securely. Print address on box so if wrappings come loose, address will not be destroyed. Wrap in heavy paper, address package, and label it, "Fragile, Handle with Care."

Types of cookies

Most cookies are categorized according to the stiffness of the dough. The softer doughs are usually dropped by the spoonful onto a baking sheet. The stiffer ones may be chilled and sliced or rolled out on a floured board. Other doughs are pressed, molded, or baked in a sided pan. The descriptions and recipes which follow are grouped according to the final handling or shaping of the dough.

Bar cookies: These are cake-cookies made of a stiff dough that is spread or pressed evenly into a pan, then baked, cooled slightly, and cut into squares or diamonds. Sometimes a meringue or special topping is baked on. Usually, however, the finished bars are sprinkled with confectioners' sugar or topped with frosting.

Bar cookies generally have a thin, delicate crust and a rich, moist eating quality. A hard, crusty top is a sure sign the dough was overmixed. Overbaking should be guarded against, too, as the bars will be dry and crumbly. Fudge-type bars are done when the surface is dull in appearance and a slight imprint remains after touching the surface with a fingertip. Cakelike bars should be baked until a wooden pick inserted in the center of the pan comes out clean. Cut in bars or squares when cooled.

Maple Nut Chews

1/3 cup butter or margarine
1/2 cup brown sugar
1/2 teaspoon maple flavoring
1 egg
1/2 cup sifted all-purpose flour
1/4 teaspoon salt
1/4 teaspoon baking powder
1/2 cup raisins
1/2 cup chopped walnuts

In a saucepan melt butter and sugar; cool slightly. Beat in maple flavoring and egg. Sift flour with salt and baking powder; stir into butter mixture. Stir in raisins and chopped walnuts; spread in a greased 8x8x2-inch pan. Bake at 350° for 25 to 30 minutes. Cool slightly before cutting into bars. Makes 16 bars.

Cereal-Peanut Bars

A no-bake cookie that tastes like a candy bar—

½ cup light corn syrup
¼ cup brown sugar
Dash salt
1 cup peanut butter
1 teaspoon vanilla
2 cups crisp rice cereal
1 cup cornflakes, slightly crushed
1 6-ounce package semisweet chocolate pieces (1 cup)

Combine syrup, sugar, and dash salt in saucepan; bring to a full boil. Stir in peanut butter. Remove from heat. Stir in vanilla, cereals, and chocolate pieces. Press into a buttered 9x9x2-inch pan. Chill 1 hour. Cut in small bars or squares. (For easy serving, store in refrigerator.) Makes about 2 dozen pieces.

Candlestick Bars

Whip up Christmas goodies quickly with mixes—

1 14-ounce package gingerbread mix
1 8-ounce can applesauce (1 cup)
½ cup raisins
½ cup chopped mixed candied fruits and peels (4 ounces)
1 14-ounce package white creamy-type frosting mix
2 tablespoons lemon juice
Gumdrops

Blend gingerbread mix and applesauce. Beat 2 minutes at medium speed with electric mixer or 2 minutes with spoon. Stir in raisins and fruit. Spread in greased 15½x10½x1-inch pan. Bake at 375° for 15 minutes. Substituting lemon juice for *half* the liquid, make frosting following label directions. Spread on cooled cookies. Cut in 1x1½-inch bars. Trim with candlesticks cut from gumdrops. Makes 8 dozen.

Bonny, bonny bar cookies

← Chewy with oatmeal, buttery-rich Scotch Teas need few ingredients and only a saucepan for mixing. They're oh so easy to bake!

Chocolate Mint Sails

Prepare one recipe of Fudge Brownies (see *Brownie* for recipe). *Or* bake 1 package brownie mix following label directions. Cool.

Combine 1 cup sifted confectioners' sugar; 2 tablespoons butter, softened; 1 tablespoon light cream; and ¼ to ½ teaspoon peppermint extract. Beat well. Tint with green food coloring. Spread over cooled brownie layer; let stand till set. Melt one 1-ounce square unsweetened chocolate with 1 tablespoon butter. Drizzle over frosting. Chill till firm. Cut in bars or triangles. Makes 2 dozen.

Scotch Teas

Combine ½ cup butter or margarine and 1 cup brown sugar in saucepan; cook and stir till butter melts. Stir in 2 cups quick-cooking rolled oats, 1 teaspoon baking powder, and ¼ teaspoon salt. Mix well. Pour into greased 8x8x2-inch baking pan. Bake at 350° for 20 to 25 minutes. Cool; cut into bars. Makes 24 bars.

Apple-Orange Brownies

Mixed in a saucepan to save bowl washing—

6 tablespoons butter or margarine
1 cup brown sugar
½ cup applesauce
1 teaspoon shredded orange peel
1 beaten egg
1 teaspoon vanilla
1¼ cups sifted all-purpose flour
1 teaspoon baking powder
½ teaspoon salt
¼ teaspoon baking soda
½ cup chopped walnuts
Orange Glaze

In saucepan combine butter and brown sugar; cook and stir till melted. Beat in applesauce, orange peel, egg, and vanilla. Sift together next four ingredients; stir into mixture in saucepan. Stir in nuts. Spread in greased 15½x10½x1-inch pan. Bake at 350° for 15 minutes. While warm, top with Orange Glaze. Makes 4 dozen.

Orange Glaze: Combine 1½ cups sifted confectioners' sugar, ½ teaspoon vanilla, dash salt, and about 2 tablespoons orange juice.

Drop cookies: One of the easiest cookies to stir and bake, drop cookies get their name from the fact that the soft dough is dropped by spoonfuls onto a baking sheet. Nuts, fruits, candies, or cereals are often added to give variety in texture and flavor. Sometimes drop cookies are frosted.

Underbaking will cause a rough spot in the center of the cookies and overbaking tends to make them dry and hard with dark, crisp edges. Drop cookies are done to perfection when they are delicately browned and the imprint made by the light touch of a finger is slightly visible.

When baking a large batch of cookies, some homemakers find the cookies spread out more than desired. Chilling the dough slightly and mounding it up when dropped will help solve the problem. Making sure the cookie sheet has time to cool between batches is another good practice to follow because the heat from the pan causes the dough to melt and spread.

Meringue cookies, sometimes called kisses, are a cross between a cookie and a confection. Depending on the consistency of the mixture, they may be dropped by spoonfuls, forced through a pastry tube, or formed into balls by hand. They often have ground nuts, coconut, crushed candy, or crisp cereal folded in before baking. Although similar to the drop cookie, the macaroon is traditionally made with almond paste. Short-cut versions using sweetened condensed milk are popular, too.

Easy Macaroons

Mix two 8-ounce packages shredded coconut, one 15-ounce can sweetened *condensed* milk (1⅓ cups), and 2 teaspoons vanilla. Drop mixture from a teaspoon onto a well-greased cookie sheet. Bake at 350° for 10 to 12 minutes. Cool macaroons slightly before removing to rack. Makes about 4 dozen macaroons.

A fruit cookie fantasia

← Party favorites include Lemon Tea Cakes with coconut crowns, moist Apple-Orange Brownies, and Date-Marmalade Pastries.

Lemon Tea Cakes

1½ teaspoons vinegar
½ cup milk
½ cup butter or margarine
¾ cup granulated sugar
1 egg
1 teaspoon shredded lemon peel
1¾ cups sifted all-purpose flour
1 teaspoon baking powder
¼ teaspoon baking soda
¼ teaspoon salt
Lemon Glaze

Stir vinegar into milk. Cream butter and sugar till fluffy. Beat in egg and peel. Sift together dry ingredients; add to creamed mixture alternately with milk, beating after each addition. Drop from teaspoon 2 inches apart on *ungreased* cookie sheet. Bake at 350° for 12 to 14 minutes. Remove at once from sheet; brush tops with Lemon Glaze. If desired, garnish with tinted coconut. Makes 4 dozen.

Lemon Glaze: Thoroughly blend ¾ cup granulated sugar and ¼ cup lemon juice.

Cocoa Drop Cookies

1 cup butter or margarine
1¾ cups granulated sugar
1 cup cottage cheese
1 teaspoon vanilla
2 eggs
2½ cups sifted all-purpose flour
½ cup unsweetened cocoa
1 teaspoon baking soda
1 teaspoon baking powder
½ teaspoon salt
Confectioners' Icing

Cream butter and sugar till fluffy. Add cottage cheese and vanilla; beat thoroughly. Add eggs, one at a time, beating well after each addition. Sift together flour, cocoa, soda, baking powder, and salt; gradually add to creamed mixture. Drop by rounded teaspoons onto greased cookie sheet. Bake at 350° about 12 minutes. Let stand briefly before removing from cookie sheet. When cool, frost with Confectioners' Sugar Icing. Makes 6½ dozen.

Confectioners' Icing: Combine 2 cups sifted confectioners' sugar, dash salt, and 1 teaspoon vanilla. Add milk until desired consistency.

Oatmeal Chip Cookies

½ cup shortening
½ cup granulated sugar
½ cup brown sugar
½ teaspoon vanilla
1 egg
1 cup sifted all-purpose flour
½ teaspoon baking soda
½ teaspoon salt
1 cup quick-cooking rolled oats
1 6-ounce package semisweet chocolate pieces (1 cup)
½ cup chopped walnuts

Thoroughly cream shortening, sugars, and vanilla. Beat in egg, then 1 tablespoon water. Sift together flour, soda, and salt; add to creamed mixture, blending well. Stir in the rolled oats, chocolate pieces, and chopped walnuts. Drop by rounded teaspoons onto a greased cookie sheet about 2 inches apart. Bake at 375° for 10 to 12 minutes. Cool slightly before removing from pan. Makes 3½ to 4 dozen.
Note: For *Polka-dot Oatmeal Crisps,* substitute one 10½-ounce package candy-coated chocolate pieces for chocolate chips and nuts.

Chocolate Yummies

1 4-ounce package chocolate pudding mix (regular type)
2 cups packaged biscuit mix
½ cup granulated sugar
1 slightly beaten egg
¼ cup milk
¼ cup butter or margarine, melted
1 teaspoon vanilla
1 3½-ounce can flaked coconut (1⅓ cups)
Refrigerated ready-to-spread creamy chocolate frosting
Walnut halves

Combine pudding mix (dry), biscuit mix, and sugar. Beat in egg, milk, melted butter or margarine, and vanilla. Stir in coconut. Drop dough from teaspoon onto an *ungreased* cookie sheet. Bake at 350° for 11 to 13 minutes. Remove cookies to cooling rack. Spread cooled cookies with chocolate frosting; top with walnut halves. Makes about 3 dozen cookies.

Crunch Cookies

Honey sweetened, spicy drop cookies—

½ cup shortening
½ cup sugar
½ cup honey
1 egg
2 tablespoons milk
. . .
1½ cups sifted all-purpose flour
1 teaspoon salt
1 teaspoon ground cinnamon
½ teaspoon baking soda
1 cup shredded wheat cereal, crumbled
½ cup chopped walnuts
1 cup raisins

Cream together shortening, sugar, honey, egg, and milk. Sift together flour, salt, ground cinnamon, and baking soda; add to creamed mixture. Stir in shredded wheat cereal, nuts, and raisins. Drop from teaspoon onto greased baking sheet. Bake at 375° till lightly browned, about 12 to 13 minutes. Cool slightly before removing cookies from baking sheet. Then cool on rack. Makes about 5 dozen cookies.

Refrigerator cookies: The dough for these cookies is shaped into rolls, wrapped, and chilled thoroughly in the refrigerator before slicing and baking. Nuts and fruits, when used, must be finely chopped so that they do not interfere with slicing the cookies. For dainty, round cookies the dough can be shaped in a washed, empty, frozen fruit-juice container from which both ends have been removed.

Because of their high shortening content, refrigerator cookie doughs stiffen when chilled. Thus, the cold rolls of dough will slice easily with a thin, sharp knife. For best results, cut the cookies by using a back-and-forth sawing motion. Pressing down on the knife while slicing may distort the cookie's shape.

Slice and bake cookies as needed. The unbaked dough can be re-wrapped and stored in the refrigerator for up to one week or placed in the freezer for up to six months. Refrigerator cookies, baked until lightly browned, will have a crisp texture.

Crisp Pecan Slices

Lemony-rich cookies to slice and bake right from refrigerator or freezer—

3/4 cup butter or margarine
1 cup sugar
1 egg
1 teaspoon grated lemon peel
1 tablespoon lemon juice
2 cups sifted all-purpose flour
1 teaspoon baking powder
1/2 teaspoon salt
1 cup finely chopped pecans

Thoroughly cream butter and sugar. Add egg, lemon peel, and juice; beat well. Sift together flour, baking powder, and salt; add to creamed mixture, mixing well. Stir in finely chopped nuts. Shape in rolls 2 inches in diameter. Chill thoroughly, about 2 hours.

Using a sharp knife, slice very thin and place on *ungreased* baking sheet. Bake at 350° till delicately browned, about 10 to 12 minutes. Cool cookies slightly before removing from pan. Makes about 5 dozen cookies.

Cherry Refrigerator Cookies

Tender slices flavored with a dash of cinnamon—

1 cup butter or margarine
1/2 cup granulated sugar
1/2 cup brown sugar
2 eggs
1 teaspoon vanilla
2 3/4 cups sifted all-purpose flour
1 teaspoon baking powder
1/4 teaspoon salt
1/4 teaspoon baking soda
Dash ground cinnamon
1 cup chopped candied cherries
1/2 cup chopped walnuts

Cream butter and sugars together till fluffy. Add eggs and vanilla; beat well. Sift dry ingredients together and stir into creamed mixture. Add cherries and nuts. Shape into rolls about 1 1/2 inches in diameter. Wrap in waxed paper or foil and chill overnight. Slice 1/4 inch thick. Place on baking sheet 1 inch apart. Bake at 375° till delicately browned, about 10 to 12 minutes. Makes 5 dozen cookies.

Quick Sandwich Cookies

1 roll refrigerated slice-and-bake sugar cookies
26 pecan halves
1/2 cup semisweet chocolate pieces

Cut cookie dough into 13 slices of about 3/4-inch thickness. Cut each slice into quarters. Place 2 inches apart on *ungreased* baking sheet; bake at 375° about 9 minutes. Remove from oven. Top *half* the cookie slices with a pecan half. Top each of the remaining cookies with several chocolate pieces. Return to oven for about 1 minute; remove from oven. Spread softened chocolate evenly over the chocolate-topped cookies. Place pecan-topped cookie atop each chocolate cookie. Makes 26 sandwiches.

Rolled cookies: These are made from a fairly soft dough which is chilled so that it is easy to handle. The dough is rolled out to the desired thickness on a lightly floured board or canvas. Cutters range from round biscuit cutters to fancy-shaped flowers, animals, or stars. Simple patterns of your own design cut from pasteboard or heavy brown paper and traced on the dough with the tip of a knife make interesting cookie shapes, too. When giant-sized cookies are wanted, a coffee can cover becomes an excellent cookie cutter.

Small amounts of chilled dough are rolled out at a time. The remainder of the dough should be returned to the refrigerator until needed. This is important because dough allowed to stand at room temperature will soften and take up more flour than necessary during rolling. Excessive re-rolling and using too much flour on the board tends to make dry, tough cookies.

Some rolled cookies are thin and crisp while others are thicker with a soft interior. Frequently, rolled cookies are folded over a filling of fruit, nuts, or frosting before baking. Sometimes the filling is spread between two baked cookies which are then put together sandwich fashion. Cookies filled before baking should be sealed well at the edges so that the filling stays inside where it belongs. Rolled and filled cookies are baked till tops are golden brown.

Mincemeat Star Cookies

1⅓ cups shortening
1½ cups granulated sugar
2 eggs
1 teaspoon vanilla
1 teaspoon grated orange peel
4 cups sifted all-purpose flour
3 teaspoons salt
2 tablespoons milk
Mincemeat Filling

Cream together shortening, sugar, eggs, and vanilla till light and fluffy. Stir in grated orange peel. Sift together dry ingredients; add to creamed mixture alternately with milk. Divide dough in half; chill.

On lightly floured surface, roll each half to ⅛-inch thickness. Cut cookies with 2¾-inch round cutter. Cut small star in centers of *half* the cookies. Place 1 heaping teaspoon Mincemeat Filling on each plain cookie. Top with a cutout cookie; press edges with fork to seal securely. Bake on greased baking sheet at 375° till a delicate brown, about 12 minutes. Makes 2½ dozen filled cookies.

Mincemeat Filling: Break one 9-ounce package mincemeat in pieces. Add 2 tablespoons granulated sugar, 2 teaspoons grated orange peel, 1 teaspoon grated lemon peel, and ¾ cup orange juice. Heat, stirring till lumps are broken; then simmer mixture about 1 minute. Cool; stir in ¼ cup chopped walnuts.

Paul Bunyan Sugar Cookies

Cream together 1½ cups butter or margarine, 1½ cups granulated sugar, 2 eggs, and 1 tablespoon vanilla till light and fluffy. Stir in 2 tablespoons milk and ½ cup raisins. Sift together 4 cups sifted all-purpose flour, 3 teaspoons baking powder, and ½ teaspoon salt. Stir sifted dry ingredients into creamed mixture, blending well. Chill 1 hour.

On lightly floured surface, roll chilled dough to ¼-inch thickness. Cut with 2-pound coffee can or lid of round canister (about 5 inches in diameter). Sprinkle tops of cookies with granulated sugar. Place cookies about 1 inch apart on *ungreased* cookie sheet. Bake at 375° till cookies are lightly browned, about 10 minutes. Remove the baked cookies from pan with wide spatula. Makes 14 large cookies.

Date-Marmalade Pastries

1 10-ounce package piecrust mix
1 3-ounce package cream cheese
1 tablespoon milk
1 pound pitted dates
1 cup orange marmalade

Blend piecrust mix, cream cheese, and milk. Divide dough in half. Roll each part to 10x12-inch rectangle on lightly floured surface. Cut with pastry wheel in 2-inch squares. Stuff dates with marmalade. Place date in center of each square and bring diagonal corners to center; seal. Bake at 400° till lightly browned, about 10 minutes. Makes 5 dozen.

Creme-Filled Cookies

6 tablespoons chilled butter
1 cup sifted all-purpose flour
2½ tablespoons light cream
¾ cup sifted confectioners' sugar
1 tablespoon butter, softened
⅛ teaspoon almond extract
1 tablespoon light cream

With pastry blender or fork, cut the 6 tablespoons butter into flour till size of small peas. Sprinkle *1 tablespoon* cream over part of mixture. Gently toss with fork; push to one side of bowl. Sprinkle *next tablespoon* cream over dry part; mix lightly. Push to moistened part at side. Repeat with remaining ½ tablespoon of cream till all is moistened. Carefully gather dough up with fingers; form in ball.

For easier handling, divide dough in half. On lightly floured surface, roll to slightly less than ⅛ inch. Cut dough in 1½-inch squares with pastry wheel. Dip one side of each cookie in sugar. Place sugar side up, ½ inch apart, on *ungreased* cookie sheet. With fork prick each cookie in parallel rows.

Bake at 375° till golden brown and puffy, about 8 minutes. Remove at once to cooling rack. When cookies are cool, sandwich with Almond Filling. Garnish with a dollop of Confectioners' Icing, if desired, and a few pieces of sliced toasted almonds. Makes 2½ dozen.

Almond Filling: Thoroughly combine confectioners' sugar, the 1 tablespoon butter, almond extract, and the 1 tablespoon light cream (or enough for spreading consistency).

Twin tiers show off Caramel Chews, Browned Butter Nuggets, Quick Sandwich Cookies, Candlestick Bars, Chocolate Yummies, and Coconut Cake Bars. (See *Coconut* for bars recipe.)

Shaped and pressed cookies: Since both of these cookies require special handling, they are considered here together. The dough is pliable and may need to be chilled if it becomes too soft to work with.

Shaped cookies are formed by hand. Small pieces of dough are rolled into a smooth ball or pencil-shaped roll with the palms of the hands. Sometimes the dough is wrapped around pieces of date, candied fruit, or nutmeats. When baked, some cookies keep their prebaked form, while others flatten slightly or crinkle on top. In many recipes the balls are flattened before baking with the bottom of a glass which has been dipped in granulated sugar or flour. Crisscross marks made with the tines of a fork make a pretty pattern, too. Or, a thumbprint in the soft dough leaves an indentation just the right size to fill with colorful jam or jelly after baking.

The dough for pressed cookies is forced through a cookie press into desired shapes and designs. Spritz are perhaps the best known of the dainty pressed cookies. The necessary equipment for making stars, Christmas trees, and assorted shapes comes with the cookie press. The manufacturer's directions should be followed when using a press. (See also *Christmas*.)

Jam Thumbprints

⅔ cup butter or margarine
⅓ cup granulated sugar
2 egg yolks
1 teaspoon vanilla
½ teaspoon salt
1½ cups sifted all-purpose flour
2 slightly beaten egg whites
¾ cup finely chopped walnuts
Strawberry preserves or currant jelly

Cream together butter and sugar until fluffy. Add egg yolks, vanilla, and salt; beat well. Gradually add sifted flour, mixing well.

Shape dough into ¾-inch balls; dip in slightly beaten egg whites. Roll in chopped walnuts. Place 1 inch apart on greased cookie sheet. Press down center of each with thumb.

Bake cookies at 350° till done, about 15 to 17 minutes. Cool slightly; remove from cookie sheet and cool on rack. Just before serving fill centers of cookies with preserves or jelly. Makes about 3 dozen cookies.

Browned Butter Nuggets

1 2⅞-ounce package whole, shelled filberts (about 2½ dozen)
½ cup butter or margarine
¼ cup sifted confectioners' sugar
½ teaspoon vanilla
1½ cups sifted all-purpose flour

Toast filberts in 325° oven for 10 minutes. Brown butter in saucepan. Remove from heat; immediately blend in confectioners' sugar and vanilla. Cool. Blend in flour. Shape a rounded teaspoon of dough around each nut to form balls. Place on *ungreased* cookie sheet.

Bake at 325° for 20 minutes. Cool slightly on cookie sheet; remove. When cool, sift additional confectioners' sugar over cookies, if desired. Makes about 2½ dozen nuggets.

Welcome world travelers

← Salute friends with a slide-viewing party. Parade Creme-Filled Cookies, jam-topped Tasty Pastries, and Chocolate Mint Sails.

Frosty Date Balls

½ cup soft butter or margarine
⅓ cup sifted confectioners' sugar
1 tablespoon water
1 teaspoon vanilla
1¼ cups sifted all-purpose flour
Dash salt
⅔ cup chopped pitted dates
½ cup chopped walnuts

Cream together butter and sugar. Stir in water and vanilla. Add flour and salt. Mix well. Stir in dates and walnuts. Roll in 1-inch balls. Place 2½ inches apart on *ungreased* cookie sheet. Bake at 300° till cookies are set but not brown, about 20 minutes. While warm, roll in confectioners' sugar. Makes about 2½ dozen.

Caramel Chews

Place 36 vanilla caramels (10 ounces) and 3 tablespoons light cream in top of a double boiler over simmering water. Heat till caramels melt; stir occasionally. Toss together 1 cup cornflakes, 2 cups crisp rice cereal, 1 cup flaked coconut, ½ cup chopped walnuts, and ½ cup raisins. Pour caramel mixture over. Mix thoroughly. With buttered fingers, press rounded tablespoons of mixture lightly into balls. Place on waxed paper. Makes 4 dozen.

Tasty Pastries

1 package active dry yeast
¼ cup *warm* water
1 10-ounce package piecrust mix
1 tablespoon granulated sugar
1 egg yolk
½ cup strawberry preserves, orange marmalade, *or* boysenberry jam

Soften yeast in warm water. Blend piecrust mix, sugar, egg yolk, and the softened yeast; mix well. Roll dough into balls the size of a small walnut. Place on *ungreased* cookie sheet. Make deep indentation in center of each ball, shaping into shells 1½ inches in diameter and ¼ inch deep. Spoon one teaspoon of jam into each shell. Let rise in warm place 1 hour.

Bake at 375° for 12 to 15 minutes. Cool slightly; remove from sheet. Makes 3 dozen.

Christmas tree, star, and Santa Claus cookies have developed into traditional holiday treats made with cookie cutters.

The cookie press eliminates the rolling step and is capable of producing a large variety of tasty, shaped cookies.

Turning the handle at the top forces dough through the desired opening. The disks can easily be switched to change the design.

COOKIE CUTTER—A utensil for cutting rolled dough into shaped cookies. Cookie cutters are similar to biscuit cutters but are usually a fancier shape.

COOKIE PRESS—A useful utensil for forming soft dough into different cookie shapes. A hollow tube holds the dough while a plunger forces the dough through a shaped opening. The design of the opening can be varied by interchanging metal disks.

COOKIE SHEET—A flat, broad metal sheet on which rolls, biscuits, cookies, and cream puffs may be baked. The thin metal from which cookie sheets are constructed, usually aluminum or tin, allows heat to be transmitted rapidly to the food being baked. Shiny sheets allow for more even browning than when the luster is lost.

When selecting cookie sheets, look for at least one turned-up edge for easy grasping and an open edge for easy removal.

COOKING WINE—A low-quality wine sold in grocery stores, often seasoned with salt making it unfit for drinking.

When wine is used in cooking, the alcohol is driven off by the cooking heat; only the wine flavor remains. For this reason,

A summer cooler

The irresistible beverage Raspberry Mint → Cooler combines lemonade, raspberries, and fresh mint. (See recipe on page 628.)

many cooks prefer to utilize one of the less expensive table wines rather than cooking wine. If only a little wine is needed, use some of the same wine that is to be served with the meal for the desired cooking purpose. (See also *Wines and Spirits.*)

COOL—To remove food from heat and to let it stand at room temperature. Many recipes specify cooling prior to adding ingredients which cannot tolerate heat.

COOLER—A tall, refreshing fruit or milk drink usually served with ice. Coolers are especially thirst-quenching on a hot day.

Raspberry Mint Cooler

Pictured on page 627—

½ cup lightly packed fresh mint leaves
¼ cup sugar
1 cup boiling water

• • •

1 10-ounce package frozen red raspberries
1 6-ounce can frozen lemonade concentrate
2 cups cold water

Combine sugar, mint leaves, and boiling water; let stand 5 minutes. Add raspberries and lemonade concentrate; stir till thawed. Add cold water and stir. Serve over ice. Makes 8 servings.

Sparkling Mint Cooler

1 10-ounce jar mint jelly (about 1 cup)
2 12-ounce cans unsweetened pineapple juice (3 cups)
½ cup lemon juice
1 28-ounce bottle ginger ale, chilled (3½ cups)

Combine jelly and 1½ cups water. Heat and stir over low heat till jelly melts; cool. Add pineapple and lemon juices; chill. To serve, place ice cubes in tall glasses; fill *half* full with fruit mixture. Fill remaining half with ginger ale. Stir to blend. Serves 10.

COOLIE PAN—Another name for the Chinese utensil, the wok. (See also *Wok.*)

COOLING RACK—A wire rack elevated to permit complete air circulation and used for cooling baked products such as cakes.

COON CHEESE—A sharp, aged Cheddar cheese with a dark rind. The interior of coon cheese is yellow in color, crumbly in texture, and sharp in flavor.

The patented method for preparing coon cheese involves higher temperatures and humidity than for other Cheddar cheeses. (See also *Cheddar Cheese.*)

COPPER—A pinkish brown metal used in kitchen utensils. Copper has been in abundant domestic use for hundreds of years. Formerly, cooking utensils were wholly copper; today, its properties are used to best advantage when copper is combined with or applied over other metals.

The most advantageous property of copper is its ability to spread heat evenly and quickly. In this respect, it is the cooking world's best heat conductor. Copper is also very ductile and malleable. For utensils, it may be drawn into very fine wire, hammered into thin sheets, and rolled, stamped, or pressed.

How copper utensils are produced: Copper is rarely used alone for household utensils. When applied to the bottom or as an inner layer of the bottom of a saucepan or skillet, the utensils' heating properties are improved vastly. In most instances, copper is electroplated onto stainless steel, a poor heat conductor. Whether a bottom layer or a core, the copper usually extends a short way up the sides of the pan so that the heat spreads evenly for uniform cooking.

How to use: The major disadvantage of using copper cookware is its tendency to tarnish on exposure to heat. Manufacturers coat some copper-bottomed utensils with a lacquer that prevents darkening. This finish, however, is not permanent and is unsightly while wearing off the pan.

Frequent cleaning of copper pans is needed to maintain attractive appearance. Dipping the copper portion in vinegar, then rubbing with salt, or using one of various copper cleaners, satisfactorily removes the thin film of copper oxide. (See *Pots and Pans, Saucepan,* and *Utensil* for additional information.)

COQ AU VIN ***(kôk ô van')***—A popular French chicken dish made with red wine (frequently red Burgundy) and usually cooked with onions, mushrooms, bacon or salt pork, herbs, and seasonings.

Coq au Vin

Typical accompaniments to serve include parslied potatoes and buttered green peas—

4 slices bacon, cut in small pieces
2 tablespoons chopped onion
1 2½- to 3-pound ready-to-cook broiler-fryer chicken, cut up
• • •
8 shallots *or* small whole onions
½ cup coarsely chopped carrots
1 clove garlic, minced
2 tablespoons brandy (cognac)
• • •
1 pint fresh mushrooms, sliced
2 tablespoons butter
3 to 4 sprigs parsley
1 medium whole bay leaf
¼ teaspoon dried thyme leaves, crushed
1 celery stalk with leaves, cut up
2 cups red Burgundy

In skillet brown bacon pieces and chopped onion; remove from skillet. Add chicken pieces and brown slowly in bacon drippings; remove chicken. Add shallots, carrot, garlic, and brandy; cook mixture about 3 minutes. Meanwhile, cook mushrooms with butter in skillet.

Make *Bouquet Garni:* In a tea ball or cheesecloth bag combine parsley, bay leaf, thyme, and celery; tie cheesecloth bag securely. Place in a 2-quart casserole. Layer chicken, vegetables, and mushrooms in casserole.

Add wine to the skillet; heat to boiling and stir to loosen the crusty brown bits. Pour mixture over casserole. Cover; bake at 350° for 2 hours. Remove Bouquet Garni. Serves 4.

COQUILLE ***(kō kil')***—An authentic or artificial scallop shell used for baking and attractively serving any number of seafood and creamed mixtures.

COQUILLE ST. JACQUES ***(-san zhäk)***—1. A French term for scallops. 2. The recipe name for scallops cooked in a rich, creamy wine sauce and baked in a coquille. Mushrooms and other shellfish are sometimes added to the scallop mixture.

The recipe title "Coquille St. Jacques" has an interesting origin. Pilgrims and crusaders who visited the Spanish shrine, St. James of Compostella, ate the scallop dish as penance instead of eating meat. The empty coquilles were then fastened to the pilgrims' hats for the journey home.

Small whole onions and sliced fresh mushrooms top well-sauced Coq au Vin, a French creation for the food connoisseur.

CORAL—The roe of female lobsters. During cooking, the roe turn coral red. This edible portion of lobster has a delicious flavor. Coral is also used to color sauces or lobster butter. (See also *Lobster*.)

CORDIAL ***(kôr' juhl)***—A name for an alcoholic after-dinner drink or liqueur. The word "cordial" is derived from the Latin word *cordialis* meaning "of or belonging to the heart." In England, it also refers to a sweet, water-mixed drink.

CORDON BLEU ***(kôr dôn blœ')***—1. The French term for blue ribbon and name of the most renowned classic French cooking school. The institution, established in Paris in 1700, was initially a girls' school until the fame of its cooking program resulted in a change in curriculum. 2. Sauced meat rolls of veal, ham, and cheese.

CORIANDER—A lacy-looking plant of the parsley family native to the Mediterranean region. The coriander plant has been nicknamed Chinese Parsley.

The flavor extracted from coriander leaves and seeds has been regarded highly throughout the centuries. Long ago, Asians used coriander in curry mixtures. Archaeological investigations have unearthed coriander seeds from Egyptian tombs. Ancient writings of Babylon refer to coriander's fragrance in the Hanging Gardens, and the Hebrews described their manna as "like coriander seed, white." In Roman and Grecian cooking, too, coriander was a very popular seasoning.

Difficulty in harvesting the crop accounts for importation rather than regional production of coriander in the United States. For successful harvesting, the seeds must be completely ripe to taste good; but at this stage of development, seeds fall to the ground at the slightest touch. Consequently, even though the coriander plant would grow easily here, production would not be economical. Therefore, the seeds are imported from Morocco, Romania, Argentina, and France.

Nationalities in Latin America, Russia, and Eastern Europe use coriander leaves in cooking. The Spanish call the leaves *cilantro*. In the United States, however, the dried fruits or seeds, white to yellow brown in color, are the only form normally available. The whole, round seeds are tiny, measuring about one-eighth inch in diameter. They may be purchased in two forms, either whole or ground.

Coriander seed has numerous commercial and household uses. It is the traditional "heart" of old-fashioned candies called comfits. The ever-popular frankfurter and sausage would be at a loss without the flavor of coriander. In addition, it is one of the major ingredients in curry powder and mixed pickling spices, and it is a flavoring agent used in gin. Coriander is also used to give scents to some perfumes.

The delightful aroma and taste—somewhat like lemon and sage—adds appealing flavor to cookies, candies, Danish pastry, and gingerbread as well as to beef or pork roasts, game, cheeses, and soups. (See *Herb, Spice* for additional information.)

Spareribs Far East

An exotic sauce for spareribs—

3 pounds pork spareribs
1/4 cup salad oil
1/4 cup soy sauce
2 tablespoons lemon juice
1 tablespoon instant minced onion
1 tablespoon coriander seed, crushed
1 tablespoon brown sugar
3/4 teaspoon hickory smoke-flavored salt
1/2 teaspoon ground cumin
1/2 teaspoon ground ginger
1/4 teaspoon pepper

If desired, cut spareribs into serving-size pieces. Place on rack in shallow baking pan. Bake at 450° for 30 minutes; drain off fat from pan. Reduce oven temperature to 350° and bake the spareribs 30 minutes longer.

Combine salad oil, soy sauce, lemon juice, onion, crushed coriander, brown sugar, smoke-flavored salt, cumin, ginger, and pepper. Spoon or brush sauce over ribs on all sides. Continue baking till ribs are tender, about 1 hour, continuing to baste them occasionally with the barbecue sauce. Makes 4 servings.

Coriander Cookies

1 cup butter or margarine
1 cup sugar
2 eggs
2¾ cups sifted all-purpose flour
4 teaspoons ground coriander
1 teaspoon baking soda
½ teaspoon cream of tartar
Dash salt
2 tablespoons water
Sugar

Cream together butter and the 1 cup sugar; add eggs and beat till fluffy. Sift together flour, coriander, baking soda, cream of tartar, and salt; blend into creamed mixture. Add water; beat well. Drop from teaspoon onto *ungreased* cookie sheet. Flatten with the bottom of a glass dipped in sugar. Bake at 375° for 8 to 10 minutes. Cool on rack. Makes 5 dozen.

CORKSCREW—A piece of equipment for removing corks from bottles. Many variations of the traditional corkscrew have been developed, but most of them work on similar principles. A sharp-pointed metal spiral is attached at right angles to the handle. The metal spiral should be thin, tapered, and sharp at the point only. If the edges are sharp, they will make the cork crumble. The spiral is inserted into the cork with a twisting motion. Removal of the cork may be facilitated by means of levers on the corkscrew.

A modern variation of the corkscrew is an instrument that injects a small amount of harmless gas through the cork into the bottle. The gas forces the cork out.

CORKY—A term for wines that have off-flavors due to defective corks. These wines are not recommended for drinking.

Spareribs Far East boasts a distinctive oriental flavor. Included in the seasoning blend is coriander seed, an aromatic member of the parsley family that tastes somewhat like a blend of lemon and sage. Shown in the mortar and pestle are whole coriander seeds.

CORN—A seed or kernel of the cereal plants that is used for food. In many countries, corn refers to the main crop: in England, it refers to wheat; in Scotland and Ireland, to rye. However, in America, corn refers to Indian corn or maize. Individual ears of the maize type of corn consist of kernels growing on cobs which are surrounded by fine silks and an outside husk.

The confusion in definition is carried through in the multitude of uses to which corn has been put. For instance, the Indians of Central America, Peru, and Mexico used corn as a food, as a fuel, as a building material, as jewelry, and also as a form of money for buying other items.

Although we must speculate as to corn's place of origin, archaeological findings point to Mexico or Central America. Wild corn did exist in Mexico prior to 3,000 B.C. Most probably, present-day varieties are descendents of this early wild corn. Unlike many other seeds, American corn is not wind-borne and does not seed itself. It has to be carried by hand and planted. It is not known exactly how corn was carried from Central America to North America, but it is known that in the late fifteenth century Columbus introduced corn kernels to the Spanish people.

In America, corn is most closely associated with American Indians who taught the early European settlers how to grow, harvest, and use corn. The Indians also taught settlers how to cook many Indian dishes. Some of these have become traditional American recipes. For example, succotash, a cooked corn and bean combination, is a recipe of the Indians.

Corn has undergone many changes throughout the years. From its former multicolored (red, white, yellow, and black) appearance, corn has been changed by hybridization to a single color variety, adaptable to a wide range of climates.

Nutritional value: Corn contributes carbohydrates to the diet, one medium ear adding about 95 calories. One-half cup canned whole kernel corn equals about 70 calories; cream-style corn adds a few more calories. Corn also contains some vitamin C, B vitamins, thiamine, and riboflavin, plus some vitamin A in the yellow varieties.

Types of corn: There are several types of corn, including field (dent), flint, flour, pop-, sweet, waxy, and pod. However, only a few are important to the homemaker.

Up until the mid-nineteenth century, field corn was the most common variety found on the dinner table. But with great strides in the cultivation of corn hybrids, sweet corn was developed and has become the most popular variety for eating.

Field corn, also called dent corn, is used mainly in the manufacture of cereals, starches, and other corn products. It is used also as animal feed. Much of the livestock and poultry in America is corn-fed.

The other major type is sweet corn, also called corn-on-the-cob. This type of corn has a high sugar content, thus, making it very good to eat. The sweet corn kernels are more tender and the ears are slightly smaller than those of field corn.

There are also other varieties of corn grown on a limited scale. They are used in the manufacturing of food and other products. These include popcorn and the tiny sweet corn ears that are used for pickling.

How to select: Sweet corn can be purchased fresh almost all year round in some areas, but the peak time for this crop is during the summer months. Because it's perishable, purchase just before using.

Choose ears that are well filled with even rows of plump, milky kernels. To find out if the kernels are milky, apply slight pressure on them. The kernels should puncture. Tiny kernels on the cob most often are immature and will lack flavor. The husk should have a fresh, green color, and the ears should be without worm damage.

Corn, either whole kernel or cream-style, is also available canned. It can be purchased frozen—on the cob, cut off the cob, or mixed with other vegetables. Pickled miniature corn-on-the-cob can be purchased in many gourmet food shops.

All-American corn on the cob

For best eating, choose sweet corn that has plump, milky kernels. Pass fluffy seasoned butters with the hot cooked corn. →

How to store: Use fresh corn as soon as possible after purchasing for best eating quality. Because the sugars in the kernel start turning to starch after it is picked, corn will lose its sweet flavor quickly, especially if stored unrefrigerated. Store it in the coolest part of the refrigerator as soon as possible after picking. If desired, the husks can be removed from the ears, then the ears can be placed in a plastic bag or wrapped in foil and refrigerated.

For out-of-season use, corn can be canned by either hot-pack or raw-pack methods, as whole kernel or cream-style corn. For whole kernel corn, the cob is not scraped. Cream-style corn is prepared by cutting only about half the kernel off the cob, then scraping the cob.

Or, corn can be frozen either on the cob or cut off. To freeze corn-on-the-cob, husk and remove silks. Wash and sort. Don't use overmature corn. Blanch small ears 7 minutes in boiling water, medium ears 9 minutes, and large ears 11 minutes. Chill in cold water, changing water frequently, allowing about the same amount of time for cooling as for blanching. To freeze the kernels, blanch corn 4 minutes, cool, then cut corn off cob. Store in moisture-vaporproof containers in the freezer.

Ways to prepare fresh corn

Corn on the cob: Remove husks, then silks with a stiff brush. Rinse and cook, covered, in small amount of boiling salted water (or cook in enough boiling salted water to cover) about 6 to 8 minutes. Don't overcook.

Foil-baked corn: Spread butter on husked corn, then sprinkle with salt and pepper. Wrap in foil. Bake at 450° about 25 minutes. Turn several times during baking. Or, cook wrapped corn (don't seal seam) on grill over *hot* coals 15 to 20 minutes, turning often.

Cut corn: Cut off just the tips from kernels with a sharp knife and scrape cobs with dull edge of knife. Cook, covered, in small amount of boiling salted water, or in milk, or butter till corn is done, 5 to 8 minutes.

How to use: The list of uses for corn is long. Consequently, there is a corn dish to suit every occasion, from a backyard barbecue corn-on-the-cob to fancy corn presented in a silver serving dish. An assortment of corn recipes would include soups and chowders, both main dish and vegetable casseroles, skillet dishes, quick breads, puddings, scallops, and relishes.

When eating corn-on-the-cob, use plastic handles and insert them in the ends of the ears of corn. Serve with plenty of butter, either plain or whipped, and pass snipped chives, salt, and pepper so each person can season to his individual taste.

Deviled Corn and Crab

1/4 cup butter or margarine
2 tablespoons all-purpose flour
1 tablespoon lemon juice
1 teaspoon prepared mustard
1/2 teaspoon salt
1/2 teaspoon Worcestershire sauce
Dash pepper
1/2 cup milk
1 7 1/2-ounce can crab meat, drained, flaked, and cartilage removed
2 hard-cooked eggs, chopped
1 17-ounce can whole kernel corn, drained
1 17-ounce can cream-style corn

• • •

1/2 cup grated Parmesan cheese
1/2 cup medium saltine cracker crumbs (about 14 crackers)
1 tablespoon butter, melted
Hard-cooked egg
Pimiento-stuffed green olives

In saucepan melt the 1/4 cup butter; stir in flour, lemon juice, mustard, salt, Worcestershire sauce, and pepper. Add milk all at once; cook and stir till mixture thickens and bubbles. Remove from heat; carefully stir in crab meat, chopped hard-cooked eggs, whole kernel corn, and cream-style corn.

Spoon into a 1 1/2-quart casserole; sprinkle cheese over top. Combine cracker crumbs and the 1 tablespoon melted butter; sprinkle over cheese. Bake at 350° till heated through, about 45 minutes. Garnish with hard-cooked egg wedges and olive slices. Makes 6 servings.

Two kinds of corn—whole kernel and cream-style—are included in the ingredient list for Deviled Corn and Crab. To make it a main dish casserole, pieces of crab are also incorporated.

Mexican-Style Hash

Yesterday's roast beef gets a flavor boost with the addition of corn and tomato soup—

In oven-going skillet cook 2 cups coarsely ground or diced cooked roast beef and 1/3 cup chopped onion in 2 tablespoons shortening till onion is tender but not brown. Add 1 1/2 cups finely chopped, peeled raw potatoes; one 12-ounce can whole kernel corn, drained; one 10 3/4-ounce can condensed tomato soup; and 1/4 teaspoon chili powder. Stir till thoroughly mixed. Cover skillet with foil. Bake at 350° for 35 to 40 minutes. Makes 4 servings.

Indian Corn Casserole

Bacon adds special flavor—

In a bowl combine 3 well-beaten eggs, 1/4 cup all-purpose flour, and 2 tablespoons sugar. Beat mixture thoroughly. Add 6 ounces sharp process American cheese, shredded (1 1/2 cups), and two 17-ounce cans whole kernel corn, drained. Cook 10 slices bacon till crisp. Drain and crumble. Stir in *3/4 of the bacon.*

Turn mixture into a 10x6x1 1/2-inch baking dish. Sprinkle remaining bacon atop. Bake at 350° till knife inserted in center comes out clean, about 30 minutes. Makes 8 servings.

Ham Succotash

2 9-ounce packages frozen cut green beans
2 17-ounce cans whole kernel corn, drained
2 17-ounce cans cream-style corn
2 cups soft bread crumbs (about 3 slices bread)
2 beaten eggs
1 tablespoon instant minced onion
2 teaspoons dry mustard
2 teaspoons dried basil leaves, crushed
1 teaspoon salt
½ pound boneless fully cooked ham sliced ½ inch thick
1 6-ounce can sliced mushrooms, drained
1 pound boneless fully cooked ham, cut into serving pieces

Add frozen beans to boiling salted water. Return just to boiling; drain. Set aside.

Combine whole kernel corn, cream-style corn, bread crumbs, eggs, instant onion, dry mustard, basil, salt, and dash pepper.

Cut the ½ pound of ham into cubes. Stir into corn mixture with drained beans and mushrooms. Turn into 3-quart casserole. Bake, uncovered, at 350° for 1 hour. Arrange ham pieces atop corn mixture. Bake, uncovered, 30 minutes longer. Makes 12 servings.

Beef and Vegetable Skillet

2 pounds ground beef
1 15-ounce can tomato sauce
1 12-ounce can whole kernel corn, undrained
1 10-ounce package frozen okra, thawed, and cut into ¾-inch pieces
1 tablespoon brown sugar
4 slices sharp process American cheese

In skillet brown meat; drain. Sprinkle with ½ teaspoon salt. Add tomato sauce, undrained corn, okra, and brown sugar. Bring to boiling; reduce heat. Cover; simmer 10 minutes. Arrange cheese slices atop. Cover; heat 3 to 4 minutes to melt cheese. Makes 8 servings.

Corn Pancakes with Chili

1 pound ground beef
1 tablespoon butter or margarine
½ envelope dry onion soup mix
2 teaspoons chili powder
¼ teaspoon garlic powder
1 16-ounce can red kidney beans
2 8-ounce cans tomato sauce
. . .
3 eggs
1 cup sifted all-purpose flour
1 tablespoon sugar
1 tablespoon baking powder
1¼ cups buttermilk
2 tablespoons butter, melted
3 tablespoons yellow cornmeal
½ cup whole kernel corn, drained
¾ cup shredded Cheddar cheese

Brown meat in 1 tablespoon butter. Stir in soup mix, chili powder, garlic powder, beans with liquid, and tomato sauce. Simmer, uncovered, 30 minutes; keep warm.

Beat eggs till light and fluffy. Sift together next 3 ingredients and ½ teaspoon salt; add to eggs. Beat till almost smooth. Stir in buttermilk and 2 tablespoons melted butter; beat just till smooth. Stir in cornmeal and corn. Bake on hot, lightly greased griddle till golden brown, using ¼ cup batter for each. To assemble, spoon ⅓ cup meat on each pancake; fold. Top each with 1 tablespoon shredded cheese. Serve hot. Makes 10 to 12 five-inch pancakes.

Corn Pancakes

Sift together 1 cup sifted all-purpose flour, 2 teaspoons baking powder, and ½ teaspoon salt. Blend 2 well-beaten eggs; ¾ cup light cream; one 17-ounce can cream-style corn; and ¼ cup butter or margarine, melted. Add to flour mixture and stir just till moistened.

Fry in greased skillet using ¼ cup batter for each pancake. Turn when top is bubbly and a few bubbles have broken. Add extra shortening as needed to fry pancakes. Makes 16 pancakes.

To serve, top with *Hard Sauce:* Cream ½ cup butter or margarine and 2 cups sifted confectioners' sugar till fluffy. Beat in 1 egg, 2 tablespoons brandy, and ¼ teaspoon vanilla. Chill. Spoon on pancakes and sprinkle with ground nutmeg. Makes 1⅓ cups sauce.

Speedy Corn Fritters

1 cup buttermilk pancake mix
½ teaspoon baking powder
1 8¾-ounce can whole kernel corn, drained
1 6-ounce can evaporated milk
Fat for frying

Combine pancake mix and baking powder. Add drained corn and evaporated milk. Stir just till blended. Drop from tablespoon into deep hot fat (375°). Fry until golden brown, about 2 minutes. Drain on paper toweling. Serve with butter, if desired. Makes about 32.

Corn Fritters

Cut off tips of kernels from 3 to 4 ears fresh corn, then scrape cobs to make 1 cup cut corn with liquid. (*Or* use one 8¾-ounce can whole kernel corn.) Drain corn, reserving liquid. Add enough milk to liquid to measure 1 cup.

Sift together 1½ cups sifted all-purpose flour, 3 teaspoons baking powder, and ¾ teaspoon salt. Combine 1 beaten egg, milk mixture, and corn. Add to dry ingredients. Mix just till moistened. Drop batter from tablespoon into deep hot fat (375°). Fry until golden brown, 3 to 4 minutes. Drain fritters on paper toweling. Serve with warm maple syrup, if desired. Makes 2 dozen fritters.

New England Corn Chowder

4 slices bacon
1 medium onion, thinly sliced
2 cups diced, peeled, raw potatoes
1 17-ounce can cream-style corn
2 cups light cream
1 tablespoon butter or margarine

In saucepan cook bacon till some of fat is fried out. Add onion; cook till bacon is crisp and onion lightly browned. Remove bacon; drain on paper toweling. (Drain off excess fat from saucepan.) To saucepan add 2 cups water, potatoes, and salt and pepper to taste; cover and simmer 20 minutes. Add corn and cream; simmer 5 minutes longer. Crumble the bacon; just before serving, add bacon bits and butter to corn mixture. Makes 6 to 8 servings.

Beef-Corn Chowder

1 10½-ounce can condensed beef noodle soup
¼ cup chopped green pepper
2 tablespoons chopped onion
1 17-ounce can whole kernel corn
½ cup cooked, diced, peeled potatoes
2 cups milk
Dash white pepper

In a saucepan combine condensed soup, green pepper, and onion. Simmer, covered, till vegetables are tender. Add corn plus liquid, potatoes, milk, white pepper, and dash salt. Cover and heat slowly just to boiling, stirring occasionally. Makes 6 servings.

New England Corn Chowder is flavored with bits of crisp-cooked bacon and onion. Serve with water biscuits, split, and toasted.

Corn-Sausage Chowder

1 pound bulk pork sausage
1 small onion, thinly sliced ($\frac{1}{3}$ cup)
$\frac{1}{3}$ cup chopped green pepper
2 17-ounce cans cream-style corn
1 12-ounce package loose-pack frozen hash brown potatoes
3 cups water
1 6-ounce can evaporated milk ($\frac{2}{3}$ cup)
4 ounces sharp process American cheese, shredded (1 cup)

In large saucepan cook sausage with onion and green pepper till meat is browned and vegetables are crisp-tender. Drain off fat. Add corn, potatoes, water, evaporated milk, and $\frac{1}{2}$ teaspoon salt. Heat to boiling. Reduce heat; simmer, covered, till potatoes are tender, about 15 minutes. Stir in cheese; heat till cheese melts. Serve immediately. Makes 8 to 10 servings.

Swiss Corn Bake

3 cups fresh corn cut from cob*
1 6-ounce can evaporated milk ($\frac{2}{3}$ cup)
1 beaten egg
2 tablespoons finely chopped onion
$\frac{1}{2}$ teaspoon salt
4 ounces process Swiss cheese, shredded (1 cup)
$\frac{1}{2}$ cup soft bread crumbs
1 tablespoon butter or margarine, melted

Cook fresh corn in 1 cup boiling salted water for 2 to 3 minutes or just till tender; drain well. Combine corn, evaporated milk, egg, onion, salt, dash pepper, and $\frac{3}{4}$ *cup* of the cheese. Turn into 10x6x1$\frac{1}{2}$-inch baking dish.

Toss bread crumbs with melted butter or margarine and the remaining $\frac{1}{4}$ cup cheese. Sprinkle over corn mixture. Bake at 350° for 25 to 30 minutes. Garnish with green pepper rings, if desired. Makes 4 to 6 servings.

*Or, use two 9-ounce packages frozen corn, cooked according to package directions and drained, *or* two 17-ounce cans whole kernel corn, drained, for the fresh cut corn.

Corn O'Brien

1 cup diced celery
$\frac{1}{4}$ cup butter or margarine
1 17-ounce can whole kernel corn, drained
$\frac{1}{4}$ cup chopped canned pimiento
$\frac{3}{4}$ teaspoon salt

In a saucepan combine celery and butter. Cook for 5 minutes. Add drained corn, pimiento, salt, and dash pepper. Cover; cook 10 minutes longer, stirring occasionally with a fork. Serve at once. Makes 6 to 8 servings.

Creamy Corn

1 3-ounce package cream cheese, softened
$\frac{1}{4}$ cup milk
1 tablespoon butter or margarine
$\frac{1}{2}$ teaspoon onion salt
1 17-ounce can whole kernel corn, drained

In saucepan combine cream cheese, milk, butter, and onion salt. Stir over low heat till cheese melts. Stir in corn; continue cooking until corn is heated through. Turn into serving dish. Trim with parsley or sprinkle with paprika, if desired. Makes 4 or 5 servings.

Corn Curry

3 tablespoons butter or margarine
1$\frac{1}{2}$ to 2 cups frozen or fresh corn cut from cob*
2 tablespoons chopped green pepper
2 tablespoons chopped onion
$\frac{1}{4}$ to $\frac{1}{2}$ teaspoon curry powder
$\frac{1}{2}$ cup dairy sour cream

Melt butter in skillet. Add corn, green pepper, onion, and curry powder. Cover; cook over low heat till vegetables are just tender, 8 to 10 minutes. Stir in sour cream. Season with salt and pepper. Heat, stirring constantly. *Do not boil* the mixture. Makes 4 servings.

*Or, use drained canned whole kernel corn or leftover corn cut off the cob. Add to cooked green pepper and onion with sour cream.

Spanish Corn Bread has double corn flavor. It starts with a corn muffin mix, then canned corn is added to the batter.

Golden Corn Fry

Good use for leftover corn-on-the-cob—

2 tablespoons butter or margarine
3 cups frozen or fresh corn cut from cob (4 to 6 medium ears)
½ cup light cream
2 tablespoons snipped chives
1 clove garlic, minced
Dash salt
Dash pepper
¼ cup shredded Parmesan cheese

Melt butter or margarine in saucepan. Add corn, cream, chives, garlic, salt, and pepper. Cover; simmer 10 to 15 minutes, stirring occasionally. Sprinkle with cheese. Remove from heat; let stand covered till cheese melts. Serve hot. Makes 4 to 6 servings.

Corn products: In addition to the fresh, frozen, and canned corn products, there are several other products made from corn. Cornstarch, corn syrup, corn oil, cornmeal, grits, popcorn, hominy, cereals, corn flour, animal feed, and laundry starch are all made with this most versatile crop. Corn is also used commercially in convenience mixes. (See also *Vegetable.*)

CORN BREAD—A quick bread made with cornmeal. It is one of the easiest breads to prepare and can be made simply with cornmeal, flour, eggs, milk, shortening, sugar, salt, and a leavening agent, such as baking powder. Some varieties are made without the flour, for example corn pone.

In addition to being a delicious hot bread to be eaten as is, corn bread can also be split and used as a base for creamed mixtures. Or, the corn bread batter can be baked atop a casserole. To achieve a different shape, bake the batter in corn stick pans for individual servings.

Corn bread can be purchased at some bakeries, or made at home from a mix or from simple ingredients. (See also *Bread.*)

Spanish Corn Bread

1 14-ounce package corn muffin mix
½ teaspoon dry mustard

• • •

1 12-ounce can whole kernel corn with peppers, drained
¼ cup finely chopped onion
1 beaten egg
¾ cup milk

Combine corn muffin mix and dry mustard. Stir in corn, onion, egg, and milk; mix just till combined. Turn batter into greased 8x8x2-inch baking pan. Bake at 400° till done, about 30 minutes. Cut into squares and serve the bread while warm.

Speedy Corn Bread Pie

Keep ingredients on hand for a quick meal—

2 15-ounce cans barbecue sauce and beef
1 8-ounce can kidney beans, drained
1 8-ounce package corn muffin mix

Combine first 2 ingredients; bring to boiling. Pour into 1½-quart casserole. Prepare corn muffin mix following package directions. Spread atop *hot* meat mixture. Bake at 400° for 20 to 25 minutes. Makes 6 servings.

Perfect Corn Bread

1 cup sifted all-purpose flour
¼ cup sugar
4 teaspoons baking powder
¾ teaspoon salt
1 cup yellow cornmeal
2 eggs
1 cup milk
¼ cup shortening

Sift flour with sugar, baking powder, and salt; stir in cornmeal. Add eggs, milk, and shortening. Beat with rotary or electric beater till just smooth. (Do not overbeat.) Pour into greased 9x9x2-inch pan. Bake at 425° till done, 20 to 25 minutes. Cut into squares.

Corn Sticks: Spoon batter into greased cornstick pans, filling ⅔ full. Bake at 425° for 12 to 15 minutes. Makes 18.

CORN CHIP—A crisp, waferlike snack made from corn. It is manufactured by cooking, soaking, and grinding white and yellow corn into a dough called *masa.* This dough is put through a press, forming its characteristic shape, then fried and salted before packaging in boxes or bags.

Other chips are made only from yellow corn. These types of chips are cut into shapes before being toasted and fried.

Corn chips make delightful snacks alone or with dips, and add special flavor and texture to prepared dishes.

Zippy Ham Dip

Beat two 3-ounce packages cream cheese, softened, with ⅓ cup milk till light and creamy. Stir in 1½ cups ground fully cooked ham; 2 tablespoons finely chopped green pepper; and 1 tablespoon prepared horseradish. Cover; chill thoroughly. Serve with corn chips as dippers. Makes 2 cups dip.

A hot salad

←Taco Salad has all the ingredients of the familiar Mexican sandwich. For extra zip add a dash of bottled hot pepper sauce.

Taco Salad

1 pound ground beef
½ envelope dry onion soup mix (¼ cup)
¾ cup water
. . .
1 medium head lettuce, torn in bite-size pieces (about 4 cups)
1 large tomato, cut in wedges
1 small onion, thinly sliced and separated in rings
¼ cup chopped green pepper
½ cup sliced ripe olives
4 ounces sharp Cheddar cheese, shredded (1 cup)
1 6-ounce package corn chips

In skillet brown ground beef. Sprinkle onion soup mix over meat; stir in the water. Simmer, uncovered, 10 minutes. In salad bowl combine lettuce, tomato, onion, green pepper, olives, and cheese; toss well. Spoon on meat; top with corn chips. Makes 4 to 6 servings.

Mexican-Style Casserole

5 pounds ground beef
4 medium onions, chopped (2 cups)
1 cup chopped green pepper
1 tablespoon chili powder
2 teaspoons dried oregano leaves, crushed
2 teaspoons salt
3 10½-ounce cans tomato purée
2 28-ounce cans tomatoes, cut up
2 16-ounce cans red kidney beans, drained
5 cups crushed corn chips (about 6 ounces)
8 ounces process American cheese, shredded (2 cups)

Divide beef, onion, and green pepper between 2 large skillets. Cook till meat is browned and vegetables are tender; drain off excess fat. Divide next 6 ingredients and *4 cups* of the chips between the 2 skillets; mix. Simmer, uncovered, for 5 minutes. Turn into *two* 13x9x2-inch baking dishes. Bake, uncovered, at 350° till hot, about 35 minutes. Sprinkle remaining corn chips and cheese atop casseroles. Bake 5 minutes longer. Makes 24 servings.

CORNED—The process of preserving foods in a salt brine solution or with coarse salt. It was originally used as a method of storing meat without refrigeration.

CORNED BEEF—The brisket, plate, or round of beef cured or pickled in a strong salt brine. All bones and extra fat are removed from the cut of meat before it is cured. The brine can either be pumped into the meat or the meat can be soaked in the brine. Other ingredients in the brine include sugar, which adds flavor, and salts called nitrates and nitrites, which affect the color of the meat. Some corned beef is grayish brown in color because nitrates were not used in the processing. Other pieces of corned beef are dark red due to the action of the nitrates. Unlike other meats that are cured, for example, ham or picnic, corned beef is not smoked.

Corned beef can be purchased with either a mild cure or a cure including spices. The spices, such as allspice, cloves, and peppercorns, and herbs, including bay leaves, are added for additional flavor. Garlic can also be added.

Corned beef contains protein and some of the B vitamins, thiamine, riboflavin, and niacin; however, thiamine is partially destroyed when the meat is cured.

Store ready-to-cook corned beef as it comes from the grocery store in its original wrapper. Place it in the refrigerator and for best eating quality, do not store for longer than a week. Freezing corned beef is not recommended for best quality.

Because it is made from less tender cuts of beef, corned beef needs long, slow cooking in liquid. Some corned beef has been made tender during processing. This pre-tenderized meat can be roasted in the oven following label directions.

Typical dishes made with corned beef are corned beef and cabbage and corned beef hash. It also makes delicious sandwiches and is used in familiar Reuben sandwiches with sauerkraut and cheese.

Corned beef not only can be purchased at the meat counter ready to cook, but it is also available canned, fully cooked. Canned corned beef hash and corned beef luncheon meat are also products that can be obtained in food stores.

Corned Beef with Sweets

1 3- or 4-pound ready-to-cook corned beef brisket
½ cup chopped onion
8 sweet potatoes, peeled
2 10-ounce packages frozen Brussels sprouts

Place corned beef brisket in Dutch oven and barely cover with water. Add onion. If seasonings are not in package, add 2 bay leaves, and 6 whole black peppercorns. Cover; simmer till almost tender, about 2½ to 3 hours.

Add sweet potatoes and cook 30 minutes more. Add frozen Brussels sprouts and cook 15 minutes longer. Remove bay leaves and serve vegetables with meat. Makes 8 servings.

Peach-Glazed Corned Beef

1 3-pound ready-to-cook corned beef brisket
1 29-ounce can peach halves
¼ cup brown sugar
¼ cup catsup
2 tablespoons vinegar
2 teaspoons prepared mustard

Place corned beef brisket in Dutch oven; add water to cover. If seasonings are not in package, add 1 bay leaf. Cover and simmer till meat is tender, about 2½ to 3 hours. Remove from heat; cool meat in cooking liquid. Remove meat; slice across the grain.

Arrange slices, overlapping, in 12x7½x2-inch baking dish. Drain peaches, reserving ¼ cup syrup. Arrange peaches around meat. Combine reserved syrup and remaining ingredients. Pour over meat. Bake at 350° for 1 hour, basting with the sauce occasionally. Serves 6.

Grilled Reubens

Spread 6 slices pumpernickel or rye bread with ½ cup Thousand Island salad dressing. Top each with 1 slice Swiss cheese, 2 tablespoons well-drained sauerkraut, thin slices cooked or canned corned beef, and a second bread slice. Butter tops and bottoms of sandwiches. Grill on both sides till hot and cheese melts. Serve hot. Makes 6 sandwiches.

Reuben Roll-Ups

1 package refrigerated crescent rolls (8 rolls)
1 8-ounce can sauerkraut, well drained
1 tablespoon Thousand Island salad dressing
8 thin slices cooked corned beef (about 4 ounces)
2 slices process Swiss cheese, cut in ½-inch strips

Unroll crescent roll dough; separate into 8 triangles. Snip drained sauerkraut in can to cut long strands; combine with salad dressing. Place one slice corned beef across wide end of triangle. Spread 2 tablespoons sauerkraut on corned beef. Top with 2 strips of cheese. Roll up, beginning at wide end of triangle. Bake on *ungreased* baking sheet at 375° till golden brown, about 10 to 15 minutes. Serve the roll-ups hot. Makes 8 servings.

Canned corned beef products make delicious and quick additions to a countless number of main dish items—from molded salads to casseroles and skillet dishes—perfect for supper. (See also *Beef*.)

For tender slices, carve corned beef brisket across grain at a slight angle, making slices ⅛ to ¼ inch thick. Carve from two sides, alternating sides for equal pieces.

Corned Beef Loaf

A main-dish salad—

In saucepan soften 2 envelopes unflavored gelatin in 1 cup tomato juice; stir over low heat till gelatin is dissolved. Add 1 cup tomato juice, 1 cup mayonnaise, 2 teaspoons lemon juice, and ½ teaspoon salt. Beat smooth with rotary beater. Chill till partially set.

Fold in one 12-ounce can corned beef, crumbled (2 cups); ½ cup chopped celery; ½ cup chopped unpeeled cucumber; and 1 tablespoon chopped onion into gelatin mixture. Pour into an 8½x4½x2½-inch loaf dish. Chill till firm. Unmold onto a platter lined with salad greens. Makes 4 to 6 servings.

Corned Beef and Noodles

Cook 4 ounces medium noodles (2 cups) according to package directions; drain. In saucepan melt 3 tablespoons butter or margarine; stir in 3 tablespoons all-purpose flour. Add 2¼ cups milk; cook quickly, stirring constantly, till mixture thickens and bubbles. Stir in 1 tablespoon prepared horseradish, 2 teaspoons salt, 1 teaspoon prepared mustard, and dash pepper; mix thoroughly.

Add one 10-ounce package frozen peas, thawed, and noodles. Turn into 10x6x1½-inch baking dish. Arrange one 12-ounce can corned beef, cut in 6 slices, over noodles. Bake at 350° for 30 minutes. Makes 5 or 6 servings.

Jazzy Hash

1 15-ounce can corned beef hash
½ cup dairy sour cream
¼ cup red Burgundy
2 beaten eggs
2 tablespoons chopped onion
1 small clove garlic, minced
1 cup soft bread crumbs
1 tablespoon butter, melted
Dash paprika

Combine first 6 ingredients and dash pepper; mix well. Spoon into 4 individual casseroles or one 8-inch pie plate. Combine remaining ingredients; sprinkle over hash. Bake at 350° for 25 to 30 minutes. Makes 4 servings.

Corned Beef Bake

1 12-ounce can corned beef, finely chopped
½ cup finely chopped green pepper
½ cup finely chopped onion
½ cup mayonnaise
Dash pepper
1 beaten egg
½ cup fine dry bread crumbs
2 tablespoons shortening
3 slices sharp process American cheese
1 10½-ounce can condensed cream of celery soup
1 8¼-ounce can mixed vegetables, drained
⅓ cup milk
3 large English muffins, halved and toasted

Combine corned beef, green pepper, onion, mayonnaise, and pepper. Shape into 6 patties. Blend egg and 1 tablespoon water; dip patties into egg, then crumbs. Brown lightly in hot shortening. Place patties in 10x6x1½-inch baking dish. Quarter cheese slices diagonally; overlap 2 triangles atop each patty. Combine soup, vegetables, and milk; heat. Pour around patties. Bake at 350° till hot, about 12 minutes. Serve on muffins. Makes 6 servings.

Corned Beef Pie

Made in a jiffy with corned beef hash—

1 15-ounce can corned beef hash
¼ cup catsup
1 slightly beaten egg
• • •
1 10-ounce package frozen baby limas
2 ounces process American cheese, shredded (½ cup)
2 tablespoons milk

Combine the hash, catsup, and egg in a bowl. Spread corned beef mixture on bottom and sides of greased 8-inch pie plate. Bake at 350° for about 30 minutes.

Meanwhile, cook limas according to package directions; drain thoroughly. Fill corned beef crust with limas. Combine shredded cheese and milk in a saucepan. Heat over *very low heat,* stirring constantly, till cheese melts. Pour cheese sauce over limas. Cut into wedges to serve. Makes 4 or 5 servings.

Quick-cooking main dish

←A well-flavored corned beef patty served atop a toasted English muffin makes Corned Beef Bake hearty enough for any supper.

CORNET—1. A name for the cone-shaped thin, waferlike pastry that is usually filled with a cream mixture. 2. A piece of paper or a thin slice of meat rolled into a cone shape. The paper cones can be used as decorating tubes. Sometimes the pastry cones are referred to as cornucopias.

CORNFLAKES—A crisp, ready-to-eat cereal made from milled corn. In the processing, sugar, salt, and malt flavoring are combined with the corn. The mixture is cooked and then rolled into flakes under many tons of pressure. At this point, the flakes are toasted at a high temperature for a very short period of time.

During processing, the cornflakes are restored to the whole corn nutritive levels. One cup of cornflakes adds about 95 calories to the diet, plus some sodium, the B vitamin, thiamine, and carbohydrates.

Cornflakes can be purchased in several package sizes, either plain or presweetened with a sugar coating. Another cornflake product that is available is the ready-to-use cornflake crumbs. They can be incorporated into meatballs, quick breads, pancakes, and desserts, or used as a coating for chicken or chops. (See also *Cereal.*)

CORN FLOUR—Cornmeal that is ground and sieved until it resembles wheat flour. Corn flour in English cookery is called cornstarch. (See also *Flour.*)

CORNISH GAME HEN—The smallest, youngest member of the chicken family, sometimes referred to as Rock Cornish Hen.

It was developed as a crossbreed between the English Cornish male chicken and the White Rock female chicken. This breed of chicken is fed for four weeks and at this time certain females are selected and put on a high-fat diet for an additional two weeks. They usually weigh 1½ pounds or less when marketed and have a small bone structure, but they are well fleshed. The meat from the Cornish game hen is light and has a delicate flavor very much like the white meat of chicken.

Cornish game hens are available year-round in the frozen food department in the supermarket. Store in the freezer, then thaw wrapped birds before cooking, either in the refrigerator or in cold water, changing the water often.

Since the bird is so young and tender, it can be roasted, broiled, or fried and is delightful when stuffed before roasting. Most often a small bird makes one generous individual serving. (See also *Chicken*.)

Rice-Stuffed Cornish Game Hens

2 1-pound ready-to-cook Cornish game hens
2 tablespoons slivered almonds
2 tablespoons finely chopped onion
⅓ cup uncooked long-grain rice
3 tablespoons butter or margarine
1 cup water
1 chicken bouillon cube
1 teaspoon lemon juice
½ teaspoon salt
1 3-ounce can chopped mushrooms, drained (½ cup)
Butter or margarine, melted

Season game hens inside and out with salt and pepper. In small saucepan cook almonds, onion, and rice in 3 tablespoons butter for 5 to 10 minutes, stirring frequently.

Add water, bouillon cube, lemon juice, and ½ teaspoon salt. Bring mixture to boiling, stirring to dissolve bouillon cube. Reduce heat; cover and cook slowly till liquid is absorbed and rice is fluffy, about 20 to 25 minutes. Stir in drained mushrooms.

Lightly stuff birds with rice mixture. Follow directions for cooking according to How to Roast Cornish Game Hens chart (see page 648). Brush with melted butter or margarine before roasting and during last 15 minutes of roasting. Makes 2 servings.

Cornish Hens Supreme

4 1- to 1½-pound ready-to-cook Cornish game hens
¼ cup butter or margarine, melted

. . .

⅓ cup sugar
1 17-ounce can fruit cocktail, drained (reserve syrup)
½ cup dry sauterne
2 tablespoons cornstarch
½ teaspoon salt
½ teaspoon grated orange peel
½ teaspoon grated lemon peel
¼ cup lemon juice

Salt inside of birds and truss. Follow directions for cooking according to How to Roast Cornish Game Hens chart (see page 648). Uncover and baste with melted butter or margarine the last hour of roasting. Serve with hot Wine Fruit Sauce. Makes 4 servings.

Wine Fruit Sauce: Caramelize sugar over low heat in heavy saucepan. Heat fruit cocktail syrup to boiling; slowly add to melted sugar. Cook and stir till dissolved. Combine wine, cornstarch, salt, and grated peels. Stir into hot syrup mixture and cook, stirring constantly, until mixture thickens and bubbles. Add lemon juice and drained fruit cocktail. Heat just to boiling. Makes 2 cups.

Grill-Broiled Cornish Game Hens

Split four 1-pound ready-to-cook Cornish game hens in half lengthwise. Season. Broil slowly, bone side down, over *medium* coals, brushing well with melted butter.

When bone side is well browned, about 20 minutes, turn skin side down. Broil till tender, about 20 to 25 minutes longer. For glaze, brush both sides with a mixture of ¼ cup canned condensed consommé and ¼ cup light corn syrup. Broil 1 or 2 minutes longer to glaze Cornish hens. Makes 4 servings.

A candlelight dinner for two

Cooked whole cranberries spooned into hollowed-out lemon cups makes the ideal trim for Rice-Stuffed Cornish Game Hens. →

How to roast cornish game hens

Rinse bird; dry. Salt cavity; stuff, if desired. Close opening with skewers; lace. Place breast up on rack in shallow pan. Brush with salad oil. Roast loosely covered 30 minutes. Uncover; roast till done, 1 hour more.

Ready-to-cook weight
1 to 1½ pounds

Oven temperature
375°

Total roasting time
1½ hours

If desired, baste occasionally with melted butter or a glaze the last hour of roasting. To test for doneness, twist drumstick. It can be twisted easily in socket when done.

Cornish Hens Burgundy

For stuffing, cook 3 tablespoons sliced green onion and tops in 2 tablespoons butter till tender. Remove from heat and stir in ¼ cup toasted slivered almonds, 3 tablespoons snipped parsley, ⅛ teaspoon salt, and dash pepper. Add ½ cup cooked long-grain rice. Toss.

Salt, lightly stuff, then truss two 1- to 1½-pound ready-to-cook Cornish game hens. Follow directions for cooking according to How to Roast Cornish Game Hens chart (see above). Uncover and baste often with Burgundy Glaze the last hour of roasting. Makes 2 servings.

Burgundy Glaze: Combine in a saucepan ½ cup red Burgundy, ½ cup currant jelly, 2 tablespoons butter, 1 tablespoon lemon juice, 2 teaspoons cornstarch, 2 teaspoons Worcestershire sauce, ½ teaspoon ground allspice, dash salt, and dash pepper. Cook till mixture thickens and bubbles. Use to glaze bird during roasting; pass remaining as sauce.

Broiled Cornish Game Hens

Split one 1- to 1½-pound ready-to-cook Cornish game hen in half lengthwise. Place skin side down in broiler pan (no rack). Brush with melted butter or margarine. Season with salt and pepper. Broil 7 inches from heat for 15 minutes. Brush occasionally with melted butter. Turn; broil till done, about 15 minutes longer. Makes 2 servings.

CORNISH PASTY—A main dish turnover filled with seasoned ground meat or meat cubes and various vegetables. One of the vegetables most often included in the flaky, pastrylike crust is potatoes.

The pasty is baked in the oven and can be eaten with the fingers, either hot or cold. This particular pasty derives its name from the town in England, named Cornwall, where it originated.

CORNMEAL—White or yellow corn that has been ground into a meal.

In modern day processing, cornmeal is made from mechanically hulled and almost completely degerminated corn. The corn is ground between heavy steel rollers to fine granules, then sieved or bolted. The medium-sized granules are called grits, the finer ones are cornmeal, and the finest granules are called corn flour. Cornmeal made by this process feels dry and granular. It will keep well because most of the germ has been removed and it can be stored, tightly covered, on the shelf in a cool, dry place.

Another processing method is stone-ground cornmeal. White or yellow corn is ground in the old-fashioned way, between stones. Sometimes it is called water-ground cornmeal. This name is a carry-over from the days when grinding stones were turned by waterpower. With this process the hull and germ are not removed, although a small amount of the hull may be sieved out of the ground corn. It feels soft to the touch and is considered by some to have a true corn flavor. Stone-ground cornmeal does not keep as well and should be stored on the refrigerator shelf because it has a higher fat content.

Some cornmeal products that are available are enriched even to the point that they contain more nutrients than the whole corn. The B vitamins, thiamine, niacin, and riboflavin are added. Yellow cornmeal also contains some vitamin A.

Cornmeal is used in various countries in typical dishes, such as *polenta,* which is mush in Italian. In America, it is used to make breads, muffins, mush, and toppings for casseroles. (See *Corn Bread, Corn Stick, Indian Pudding, Mush, Scrapple* for additional information.)

Yankee Bacon Bake

½ pound sliced bacon
½ cup cornmeal
2 cups milk
½ cup sifted all-purpose flour
1 tablespoon sugar
1 teaspoon baking powder
½ teaspoon salt
3 well-beaten egg yolks
3 stiffly beaten egg whites

Quarter bacon slices. Cook till crisp; drain. Mix cornmeal with 1 *cup* of the milk. Cook till thickened; remove from heat. Sift together flour, sugar, baking powder, and salt; blend into cornmeal. Mix in remaining milk and egg yolks; fold in egg whites and crisp-cooked bacon. Bake in greased 2-quart casserole at 325° about 1 hour. Makes 6 servings.

CORN MUFFIN—A simple, quick bread made with cornmeal and baked in individual portions. Sometimes this muffin is referred to as a cornmeal muffin.

Variations of corn muffins can be made by adding a few ingredients. Crumbled, cooked bacon or canned corn can be added to the batter before turning into muffin cups. Or, other flavors, such as molasses, can be incorporated into the batter.

To make preparation of these muffins even easier, there are several simple-to-prepare mixes available. These mixes can also be used as a recipe ingredient, such as in main dish toppers. (See also *Muffin.*)

Bacon-Chive Corn Muffins

1 14-ounce package corn muffin mix
2 teaspoons snipped chives
6 slices bacon, crisp-cooked, drained, and crumbled

Prepare muffin mix according to package directions. Fold in chives, dash pepper, and bacon. Turn into 12 greased 2¾-inch muffin pans and bake at 400° till done, 15 to 17 minutes. Serve hot. Makes 12 muffins.

Molasses Corn Muffins

½ cup shortening
½ cup sugar
2 eggs
½ cup molasses
1 cup milk
1 cup sifted all-purpose flour
3 teaspoons baking powder
½ teaspoon salt
½ cup yellow cornmeal
1½ cups whole bran

Cream shortening and sugar. Beat in eggs, one at a time. Stir in molasses and milk. Sift together flour, baking powder, and salt; stir in cornmeal and bran. Add to creamed mixture, stirring just till blended. Fill paper bake cups in muffin pans ⅔ full. Bake at 375° till done, 22 to 24 minutes. Makes 18.

Sausage-Muffin Bake

1 pound bulk pork sausage
1 16-ounce can whole cranberry sauce
1 medium orange, peeled and cut up
1 8-ounce package corn muffin mix

Brown sausage, breaking up into small pieces; drain. Spread meat in 8x8x2-inch baking dish. Top with cranberry, then with orange. Prepare muffin mix following package directions. Pour over fruit; spread to edges. Bake at 375° for 35 to 40 minutes. Makes 6 servings.

CORN OIL—A golden yellow oil extracted from the germ of the corn kernel. It is odorless and flavorless, making it useful either as a salad or cooking oil. Corn oil has a high smoke point (the temperature at which fat breaks down), so it is excellent for deep-fat frying and fondue cookery. It is used in manufacturing margarines. (See *Fat, Oil* for additional information.)

CORN OYSTER—A fritter made with corn, cooked on a griddle. (See also *Fritter.*)

CORN PONE—A type of plain, unsweetened, corn bread usually made in oval or stick-like shapes. Originally they were made by the Indians who baked them in the ashes of a fire and called them *apones*. Early settlers, however, changed the name and cooked them over the fire. Now, they are most popular in the South.

CORN POPPER—1. A long-handled utensil made of wire used for popping corn over direct heat. 2. An electric appliance with a base containing the heating element, a pan for the fat and corn, and a cover.

CORN PUDDING—A custardy vegetable mixture made with fresh or canned corn that is tested for doneness like a baked custard.

Corn Pudding

3 slightly beaten eggs
2 cups drained cooked or canned whole kernel corn
2 cups milk, scalded
⅓ cup finely chopped onion
1 tablespoon butter, melted
1 teaspoon sugar

Combine eggs, corn, milk, onion, butter, sugar, and 1 teaspoon salt. Pour into greased 1½-quart casserole. Set dish in shallow pan. Fill pan to 1 inch with hot water. Bake at 350° till knife inserted halfway between center and edge comes out clean, about 40 to 45 minutes. Let stand 10 minutes at room temperature before serving. Makes 6 servings.

Quick Corn Pudding

Combine one 17-ounce can cream-style corn and one 10½-ounce can condensed cream of chicken soup. Stir in 3 well-beaten eggs. Add 1 tablespoon instant minced onion and dash pepper. Pour into a 1½-quart casserole. Set dish in shallow pan. Fill pan to 1 inch with hot water. Bake at 325° till knife inserted halfway between center and edge comes out clean, about 1¼ hours. Makes 6 servings.

CORN RELISH—A tangy side dish made with corn and served as a meat or main dish accompaniment. It often includes other vegetables and may be thickened slightly. Sometimes corn relish has a sweet-sour flavor. (See also *Relish.*)

Corn Relish

⅓ cup sugar
1 tablespoon cornstarch
1 teaspoon instant minced onion
1 teaspoon turmeric
½ teaspoon celery seed
¼ cup vinegar
1 12-ounce can whole kernel corn
2 tablespoons finely chopped green pepper
1 tablespoon finely chopped canned pimiento

In saucepan combine first 7 ingredients and ¼ cup water. Cook and stir till mixture thickens and bubbles. Stir in the green pepper and pimiento. Chill. Makes 1¾ cups.

Peppy Corn Relish adds a colorful note to any relish tray and especially sparks the flavor of grilled franks or hamburgers.

CORNSTARCH—A white, powdery substance refined from corn and used as a thickener for puddings, sauces, pie fillings, and gravies. When cornstarch is used, the thickened product has a more translucent appearance than when it is thickened with flour. Cornstarch in a reduced amount can be substituted for the flour used to thicken some sauces and gravies. The substitution is one tablespoon cornstarch equals two tablespoons flour.

When cooking with cornstarch, clumping in hot liquids can be prevented by mixing the cornstarch with sugar or a little cold liquid before adding it to the hot mixture. A cornstarch-thickened mixture should be stirred constantly until it begins to thicken. Then it should be stirred as little as possible and cooked long enough for the raw starch flavor to disappear and the mixture to take on a clear appearance. The mixture should not be overcooked.

Acids such as vinegar or lemon juice affect the thickness of the mixture and should be added after the cornstarch is completely cooked and removed from heat.

CORN STICK—A corn bread-type mixture that is baked in special heavy metal pans which are shaped like ears of corn.

Double Corn Sticks

In a bowl sift together 1 cup sifted all-purpose flour, 2 tablespoons sugar, 2 teaspoons baking powder, and 3/4 teaspoon salt. Stir in 1 cup yellow cornmeal till blended.

Blend 1 well-beaten egg, one 8 3/4-ounce can cream-style corn, 3/4 cup milk, and 2 tablespoons salad oil. Add to dry ingredients and stir just till moistened.

Preheat corn-stick pans in oven, then grease generously. Fill pans 2/3 full. Bake at 425° for about 20 minutes. Makes about 18 corn sticks.

CORN SUGAR—A granulated sugar derived from cornstarch which is broken down by acids or enzymes into sugar, then purified and dried. It is also referred to as glucose and has less sweetening power than regular sugar. (See also *Sugar*.)

Bake a batch of Double Corn Sticks for lunch or supper and serve them with a spicy, chili-type mixture—better have plenty for seconds! Next time, try corn sticks from a mix.

CORN SYRUP—A thick, clear, sweet liquid made by converting cornstarch into syrup. Corn syrups vary in color from a light crystal-clear to dark. The darkest color indicates the strongest flavor.

Corn syrup is a carbohydrate; therefore, it supplies energy for the body's activities. A tablespoon of corn syrup contains approximately 60 calories.

Both light and dark corn syrup can be purchased in pint and quart containers. At home, store these on the cabinet shelf; just be sure the cap is screwed on securely.

There are many uses for corn syrup as a topping and as an ingredient in recipes. As a topping, it goes well with pancakes, waffles, French toast, and ice cream. Sometimes, corn syrup mixtures are poured over buns and sweet rolls for a topping, adding texture and flavor.

When used as an ingredient, corn syrup gives food body, a shiny appearance, and flavor. Several characteristics of corn syrup make it especially good to use in candy. The syrup is not as sweet as granulated sugar; therefore, the candy does not become overly sweet. And because the syrup does not crystallize as easily as sugar, it helps to control the reaction of the ingredients in candy making—fudge can be made creamy and smooth, taffy soft and chewy, and brittles crisp and nonsticky.

Other examples of foods commonly made with corn syrup are pies, baby formulas, punches, and jams. (See also *Syrup*.)

Butterscotch Swirls

1 package active dry yeast
2¼ to 2¾ cups sifted all-purpose flour
¾ cup milk
½ cup sugar
¼ cup shortening

• • •

2 tablespoons butter or margarine, softened
½ teaspoon ground cinnamon
1 6-ounce package butterscotch pieces
¼ cup light corn syrup
2 tablespoons butter or margarine
½ cup chopped walnuts

In large mixer bowl, combine active dry yeast and 1¼ *cups* flour. Heat milk, ¼ *cup* sugar, shortening, and 1 teaspoon salt just till warm, stirring occasionally to melt shortening. Add to dry mixture in bowl. Beat at low speed with electric mixer for ½ minute, scraping sides of bowl constantly. Beat 3 minutes at high speed. By hand stir in enough of the remaining flour to make a soft dough. On lightly floured surface, knead 8 to 10 minutes. Place in greased bowl, turning once to grease surface. Cover; let double in warm place (about 1½ hours). Punch down; let rest 10 minutes.

Roll to 16x8-inch rectangle. Spread with the 2 tablespoons soft butter. Mix the remaining sugar and cinnamon; sprinkle over buttered rectangle. Roll lengthwise; seal. Cut in 1-inch slices. Place cut side down on greased 9x9x2-inch baking pan. Drizzle with Butterscotch Topping. Cover rolls; let double, about 40 minutes. Bake at 350° till done, about 30 minutes. Cool 2 to 3 minutes; invert on board.

Butterscotch Topping: Combine butterscotch pieces, corn syrup, the 2 tablespoons butter, and 2 tablespoons water. Melt over low heat, stirring occasionally. Cool. Add nuts.

CORNUCOPIA ***(kôr' nuh ko' pe uh)***—A container shaped like a horn or cone. A cornucopia made of pastry and filled with whipped cream makes an unusual dessert.

COS LETTUCE—Another name for romaine. (See also *Romaine.*)

COSTMARY ***(kost' mâr' ē)***—An herb with a sweet, minty, or lemony fragrance and a bitter, lemony flavor. The plant grows to three feet in height, has daisylike flowers, and long, slender, green leaves.

Mild cottage cheese goes with chives.

Cheese-Fruit Relish, a blend of cottage cheese, grapes, and pistachio nuts, is a modern version of the "curds and whey" Little Miss Muffet ate before her encounter with the spider.

Formerly, costmary had many diversified uses. In the Middle Ages, it was used to flavor ales and beers; thus, the name alecost was also given to the herb. The long, slender leaf has been popular as a bookmarker and for perfuming linens.

Today, costmary is used in salads and for flavoring. It adds a minty, lemony flavor to meats, peas, potatoes, beverages, and stuffings. (See also *Herb*.)

CÔTELETTE ***(kōt let')***—A French term meaning chop or cutlet; for instance, *côtelette de veau* means veal cutlet.

COTTAGE CHEESE—A white, soft, unripened (fresh) cheese with a slightly acidic, yet delicate flavor.

Although this form of cheese was probably one of the first made, its exact origin is unknown. However, the origin of its name is clear. Because of the simple processing involved, cottage cheese has been made for centuries by homemakers throughout the world in their cottages.

Commercial processing of cottage cheese begins with coagulation of pasteurized skim milk. When firm, the cheese is cut into either large or small cubes, then heated and stirred. The whey (watery part of milk) must be drawn off, and the cubes or curds washed with cold water. This action cleans and firms them. The curds are then salted lightly. Cream is added if cream-style cottage cheese is to be made.

To comply with federal standards, cream-style cottage cheese must have at least four percent milk fat. One tablespoon of cream-style has 18 calories compared to 14 in dry cottage cheese. Both the cream and dry types supply protein, minerals, calcium, and B vitamins in the diet.

Cream-style and dry cottage cheeses are available in supermarkets. The cream-style may also be purchased mixed with chives, fruit, or vegetables. The selection of curd size depends on personal preference. Either large or small curds can be used unless one type is specifically called for as a recipe ingredient.

Because the high moisture content of cottage cheese makes it quite perishable, always purchase it from stores that rotate their stock frequently. Refrigerate as soon as possible, being sure it's tightly covered. Use the cheese within a few days.

Cottage cheese can be eaten plain or used as an ingredient. Plain cottage cheese makes a good low-calorie snack or salad. Sugar, spices, and fresh, crisp vegetables may be added for additional flavor and texture contrast. As an ingredient, this cheese combines well with other foods for dips, appetizers, soups, salads, main dishes, and desserts. Cottage cheese is a basic ingredient in such dishes as lasagne and cheesecake. (See also *Cheese*.)

Cheese-Fruit Relish

1 16-ounce carton large curd cream-style cottage cheese, drained
1 cup halved seedless green grapes
2 tablespoons coarsely chopped pistachio nuts
1/3 cup mayonnaise or salad dressing
1/4 teaspoon salt

Combine all ingredients; mix together lightly. Chill. Serve in relish dish or spoon into lettuce cup placed in the center of a fruit platter. Makes about 2 2/3 cups.

Cottage Cheese Slaw

1/2 cup cream-style cottage cheese
1/2 cup mayonnaise or salad dressing
2 tablespoons vinegar
1/2 teaspoon caraway seed
1/2 teaspoon onion juice
1/4 teaspoon Worcestershire sauce
8 cups shredded cabbage, chilled

Blend together cottage cheese, mayonnaise, vinegar, caraway, onion juice, and Worcestershire sauce. (For stronger caraway flavor, chill mixture several hours.) Just before serving, toss dressing with cabbage. Serves 8 to 10.

Berry-Patch Salad

2 medium cantaloupes, chilled
1 12-ounce carton cream-style cottage cheese
1 8 3/4-ounce can pineapple tidbits, chilled and drained

. . .

1/2 cup hulled and halved fresh strawberries
1/2 cup fresh red raspberries

Cut cantaloupes in half crosswise; remove seeds. Combine cottage cheese and pineapple. Spoon into melon halves. Top with strawberries and raspberries. Serves 4.

Lemon Cheesecake

Crumb crust
1 cup sugar
2 envelopes unflavored gelatin
1/4 teaspoon salt
1 6-ounce can evaporated milk
2 beaten egg yolks
1 teaspoon grated lemon peel

. . .

2 12-ounce cartons cream-style cottage cheese, sieved
2 tablespoons lemon juice
1 teaspoon vanilla

. . .

2 egg whites
1 cup whipping cream

Make *Crumb Crust:* Combine 1 cup zwieback crumbs, 1/4 cup sugar, 3/4 teaspoon ground cinnamon, 1/4 teaspoon ground nutmeg, and 1/4 cup butter, melted. Mix till crumbly. Reserve 1/4 cup; press remainder on bottom and sides of buttered 9-inch springform pan. Chill.

In a saucepan, combine 3/4 *cup* sugar, gelatin, and salt. Stir in evaporated milk, then egg yolks. Cook and stir over low heat till gelatin dissolves. Add lemon peel; cool at room temperature for 30 minutes. Stir in cottage cheese, lemon juice, and vanilla. Chill, stirring occasionally, till mixture mounds. Beat egg whites to soft peaks; gradually add 1/4 cup sugar, beating to stiff peaks. Whip cream; fold egg whites and cream into gelatin mixture. Pour into chilled crust; sprinkle with reserved crumbs. Chill overnight. Serves 8.

Chilled Tomato-Cheese Soup

1 $10\frac{3}{4}$-ounce can condensed cream of tomato soup
2 cups light cream
1 teaspoon prepared horseradish
1 teaspoon lemon juice
Bottled hot pepper sauce
½ cup cream-style cottage cheese

Combine tomato soup, cream, horseradish, lemon juice, and a few dashes hot pepper sauce. Beat till well blended. Stir in cottage cheese, ½ teaspoon salt, and dash pepper; chill. Ladle into chilled bowls; sprinkle with chopped onion tops or chives, if desired. Serves 4 to 6.

COTTAGE FRIED POTATOES—Boiled potatoes which are sliced, then fried till crisp. They are also called home fries.

Cottage Fries

Cook potatoes in jackets; peel. Slice or dice. Fry in hot fat till brown and crisp, turning frequently. Season with salt and pepper.

COTTAGE PUDDING—A pudding of plain cake topped with a sauce. It usually consists of yellow cake covered with a fruit or hard sauce. (See also *Dessert*.)

Top warm cake, full of mincemeat and dates, with fluffy vanilla sauce and serve immediately. Mincemeat fans will enjoy Mince Cottage Pudding the year-round for dessert or snacks.

Mince Cottage Pudding

½ cup boiling water
½ cup finely snipped pitted dates
½ cup butter or margarine
½ cup brown sugar
2 eggs
2 cups prepared mincemeat
2¼ cups sifted all-purpose flour
3 teaspoons baking powder
1 teaspoon salt
¼ teaspoon ground nutmeg
¼ cup chopped nuts
Vanilla Sauce

Pour water over dates; cool. Cream butter and sugar till light. Add eggs, one at a time, beating well after each. Add mincemeat and dates to creamed mixture. Sift flour, baking powder, salt, and nutmeg together; mix with creamed mixture just till blended. Stir in nuts. Pour into greased and floured 13x9x2-inch baking dish. Bake at 350° till done, about 35 to 40 minutes. Cut into squares. Serve warm with Vanilla Sauce. Makes 12 servings.

Vanilla Sauce: Beat 3 egg yolks with ¾ cup sifted confectioners' sugar, 1 teaspoon vanilla, and dash salt till thick and yellow. Whip 1 cup whipping cream; fold whipped cream into sauce. Chill. Stir before serving.

Cottage Pudding

½ cup shortening
¾ cup sugar
1 egg
¼ teaspoon lemon extract
1¾ cups sifted all-purpose flour
2½ teaspoons baking powder
½ teaspoon salt
⅔ cup milk

• • •

½ cup sugar
4 teaspoons cornstarch
Dash ground nutmeg
2 beaten egg yolks
2 tablespoons butter or margarine
½ teaspoon grated lemon peel
2 tablespoons lemon juice

Cream together shortening and the ¾ cup sugar; add egg and lemon extract. Beat well. Sift together flour, baking powder, and salt. Add dry ingredients to creamed mixture alternately with milk, beating after each addition. Bake in lightly greased and floured 9x9x2-inch baking pan at 350° till cake tests done, about 40 to 45 minutes.

Meanwhile, mix the ½ cup sugar, cornstarch, dash salt, and nutmeg in saucepan. Gradually stir in 1 cup water. Cook and stir over low heat till thickened and bubbly. Stir a little hot mixture into beaten egg yolks; return to hot mixture. Cook and stir 1 minute. Remove from heat. Add butter, lemon peel, and lemon juice; blend. Serve sauce over warm cake.

COTTONSEED OIL—A clear, yellow oil with a nutlike odor extracted from the seed of cotton plants. After the oil has been removed from the seed, it must be refined. This process yields a pure, bland oil.

Cottonseed oil is used to make shortening, margarine, salad oil, salad dressing, and mayonnaise. It can also be used as a preservative, especially in canning fish.

Salad oils are available as blends of several oils or as a pure cottonseed oil. Both types are suitable for making salad dressings, panfrying, and deep-fat frying. (See *Fat, Oil* for additional information.)

Carve country-style hams by slicing either lengthwise or across the grain. Each slice should be paper-thin for flavor is very rich.

COULIS ***(ku' li)***—A thick sauce or soup made from the juices which come from meat, fish, or poultry during cooking. These are strained and thickened to make the coulis. It can also be made with a meat or fish purée rather than the juice.

COUMARIN ***(kōō' muh rin)***—White crystals which have a vanillalike odor and a burning taste. The substance is extracted from the tonka bean and other plants or made synthetically. Coumarin is used to make imitation vanilla and perfume.

COUNTRY-STYLE HAM—Specially cured and aged hams. Country-style hams are part of the Southern tradition and were developed by early settlers to keep during the hot summer months without refrigeration. They are processed in much the same way as Smithfield and Virginia-style hams with curing, smoking, and hanging.

Country-style hams need slow cooking. They must be scrubbed or trimmed, soaked, and simmered before browning in the oven and glazing. (See also *Ham.*)

COUPE ***(kōōp)***—1. A dessert made with ice cream. 2. A stemmed glass with a wide, deep bowl. 3. A rimless plate.

A coupe dessert resembles a sundae or a parfait. Toppings of a sauce, fruit, brandy, liqueur, or whipped cream are mixed with the ice cream, poured over it, or arranged in alternate layers. However, these desserts are assembled in a coupe-type glass rather than the tall parfait or sundae dish. Garnishing with candied flowers, candied fruit, or chopped nuts completes the fancy dessert or refreshment. (See *Dessert, Ice Cream* for additional information.)

Cranberry-Marshmallow Freeze

Pour marshmallow creme over top for coupe—

1 16-ounce can whole cranberry sauce
1 7-ounce jar marshmallow creme

. . .

½ cup whipping cream
1 tablespoon lemon juice
Marshmallow creme

In small mixer bowl, beat cranberry sauce into marshmallow creme. Turn into 3-cup refrigerator tray and freeze till firm. Whip cream. Remove frozen mixture to chilled mixer bowl and break into chunks. Add lemon juice and beat till fluffy. Fold in whipped cream. Return to tray; freeze firm. Makes 1 quart.

Serve in coupe-type glasses topped with additional marshmallow creme.

Cinnamon-Berry Coupe

1 teaspoon ground cinnamon
1 quart vanilla ice cream
1 pint fresh strawberries, hulled and sliced
6 tablespoons sugar
1 teaspoon grated orange peel
½ teaspoon grated lemon peel
2 tablespoons orange juice
2 teaspoons lemon juice
1 10-ounce package frozen raspberries, thawed
4 teaspoons cornstarch

Stir cinnamon into ice cream; freeze till firm in refrigerator tray. Combine sliced strawberries, *3 tablespoons* sugar, orange and lemon peel, and orange and lemon juices; chill. Sieve raspberries with syrup.

In saucepan, combine remaining sugar and cornstarch. Add raspberry purée; cook and stir till thickened and bubbly. Remove from heat; add strawberry mixture. Chill.

To serve, alternately layer cinnamon ice cream and berry mixture into coupe-type glasses, ending with ice cream. Serve immediately or return to freezer. Makes 6 servings.

COURT BOUILLON—A broth used in place of water to poach fish or vegetables. The broth consists of onion, carrot, herbs, seasonings, and water or wine, simmered and strained. The liquid can be used, not only for cooking fish and vegetables, but also in making soup and stock.

COUSCOUS—A North African dish containing cracked wheat. (See also *Wheat.*)

COWPEA—An edible bean also known as black-eyed pea. (See also *Black-Eyed Pea.*)

CRAB—A shellfish prized for its delicate, sweet meat. The crab has a flat body shaped in an oval or triangle, five pairs of legs, and a hard shell. A tail which folds up under the body distinguishes it from lobster and shrimp. One of the most unusual characteristics of the crab is its method of locomotion. These active creatures run and crawl sideways.

Crabs are found in salt water and sometimes in fresh water. Primarily, they live in shallow bays, sounds, and mouths of rivers along the Atlantic, Gulf, and Pacific coasts. Only occasionally are they found in the open sea.

The life cycle of a crab begins as a tiny egg. When the egg hatches, the baby measures only 1/25 of an inch and looks like a question mark. As it grows, the crab sheds its shell or "molts" many times. Each time the crab molts, it increases about a third in size. Full maturity is reached and molting ceases after 12 to 14 months. If not caught, a crab may live to three years of age, but few surpass this age.

Crabs are captured with pots, with wire traps on the bottom of a bay, or with baited lines. Often, in winter, crabs are dredged from the floor of a bay where they are hibernating. Once caught, these crabs are kept alive until time for cooking either by the consumer or processing plant. Live crabs, packed in seaweed and kept cold, are flown to markets all over the United States in limited quantities.

The majority of crabs that are caught are sent to processing plants. They are kept alive under carefully controlled temperatures until time for processing. Within seconds of being killed, the crabs are eviscerated and cooked. Immediately, the flesh is extracted or sections which remain in the shell, such as claws, are prepared. Then the meat is packaged, frozen, or canned and ready for market.

Nutritional value: Crab meat is a good source of protein and contains some minerals and B vitamins. If the crab meat is cooked by steaming, its meat will also have vitamin A. Each ½-cup serving of crab meat averages approximately 90 calories. One average serving of fried soft shell crab will contain 185 calories.

Types of crab: There are countless types of crabs inhabiting the American coastal waters. The most familiar are the blue, Dungeness, king, and rock crabs because they are the ones caught and marketed in the largest numbers. These four have the following characteristics and features.

Blue crabs from the middle and south Atlantic and Gulf coasts are an olive green in color. Only the tops of the claws have a blue coloring, despite the name. These crabs weigh from ¼ to 1 pound.

Dungeness crabs are caught along the Pacific coast from Monterey Bay north to Alaska. They are reddish in color and weigh from 1½ to 3½ pounds. The Dungeness meat, rich and distinctive in flavor, is composed of short, tender fibers.

King crabs from Alaska are large, weighing from 6 to 24 pounds, and measuring as much as six feet in length. Long, coarse fibers make up the white, tender meat.

Rock crabs are native to both the New England and California coasts. They are small, weighing only ⅓ to ½ pound, and have brownish colored meat.

Other types of crabs include the buster, stone, hermit, fiddler, robber-palm, spider, and shore. These are found in various regions and yield good meat.

Soft-shell crabs are not a type of crab, but rather a crab which has just shed its hard shell and has not yet grown another.

How to select: A large selection of live crabs and fresh, frozen, and canned crab meat is available in American markets.

Live crabs and fresh crab meat, although available primarily near the coasts, are flown to other sections of the country. Live crabs are usually chilled and packed in seaweed. Select those which are active and have a fresh sea smell. Fresh meat is more common on the markets than is live crab. This meat has been cooked, picked from the shell, and chilled.

Toss this salad at the table

Bring Crab-Artichoke Luncheon Salad to → the table arranged in an attractive design. Top with the creamy salad dressing and toss.

Frozen crab meat comes in several forms. It may be cooked or uncooked, in the shell or picked from the shell. Packages of parts, such as legs or cocktail crab claws, are also available.

Pasteurized crab meat is sold in cans. This is cooked and ready to eat. Be sure to refrigerate until ready to use.

Canned crab meat is also available. The types available are lump, flake, lump and flake, or claw. Lump meat consists of choice nuggets of white meat from the body. This style is attractive in cocktails and salads. Flaked meat consists of small pieces from the body that are good for casseroles and dips. A lump and flake combination is used for salads, sandwiches, and casseroles. The brownish claw meat does not look as attractive as other forms, but is quite flavorful. It is also cheaper than other forms of crab meat.

The various forms of crab meat are usually interchangeable in recipes. Selection depends on availability, personal preference, cost, and the use intended.

Buy one medium or two small crabs for each person if served whole. Four pounds of crabs with shells will yield about one pound of meat. An average serving per person is about one-fourth pound.

How to store: Live crabs should be cooked immediately. Keep the meat iced or refrigerated if it will be used in one or two days. To prolong storage time, cooked crab meat can be kept frozen for one month.

How to prepare: Canned crab meat requires little preparation. Simply drain and remove bits of cartilage and shell from the meat. Frozen crab meat should be thawed in its original wrap in the refrigerator. Boil or steam commercially frozen meat if it has not been cooked.

Live crabs are cooked in much the same way as are lobsters. They should be alive until the moment of cooking to insure freshness and quality. Crabs can be killed just before cooking or plunged into boiling water—a quick and easy method. Boil crabs about eight minutes per pound or steam about 30 minutes.

To open cooked crabs, crack the shell with a mallet. Then, pull off the back, remove the gills, and break the body in half. Remove the "butter" substance and save for soup or dressing, if desired. Rinse with cold water and pick out the body and claw meat with a nut picker.

Crab meat can be eaten with melted butter or used in hot or cold salads, dips, sandwiches, appetizers, cocktails, and casseroles. (See also *Shellfish.*)

Hot Crab Cocktail Spread

Thoroughly combine one 8-ounce package cream cheese, 1 tablespoon milk, and 2 teaspoons Worcestershire sauce. Add 2 tablespoons chopped green onion and one 7½-ounce can crab meat, drained, flaked, and cartilage removed. Turn into greased 8-inch pie plate. Top with 2 tablespoons toasted slivered almonds. Bake at 350° for 15 minutes. Keep spread warm while serving. Spread on crackers.

Crab Supper Pie

1 cup shredded natural Swiss cheese (4 ounces)
1 *unbaked* 9-inch pastry shell
1 7½-ounce can crab meat, drained, flaked, and cartilage removed
2 green onions, sliced (with tops)
3 beaten eggs
1 cup light cream
½ teaspoon grated lemon peel
¼ teaspoon dry mustard
Dash mace
¼ cup sliced almonds

Sprinkle cheese evenly over bottom of pastry shell. Top with crab meat; sprinkle with green onion. Combine eggs, light cream, ½ teaspoon salt, lemon peel, dry mustard, and mace. Pour over crab meat. Top with sliced almonds. Bake at 325° till set, about 45 minutes. Remove from oven and let stand 10 minutes before slicing and serving. Makes 6 servings.

A version of Quiche Lorraine

Add variety to family meals or impress company with Crab Supper Pie, a blend of mildly seasoned cheese, cream, and crab meat. →

Deviled Crab Meat Imperial

¼ cup butter or margarine
¼ cup minced green pepper
¼ cup minced onion
¼ cup minced mushrooms
2 tablespoons minced pimiento
1 tablespoon chopped shallots
2 tablespoons all-purpose flour
2 cups light cream

• • •

1 teaspoon salt
Dash pepper
½ teaspoon dry mustard
1 teaspoon Worcestershire sauce
2½ cups flaked crab meat
2½ cups dry white bread crumbs
1 cup hollandaise sauce

Melt butter in skillet. Add green pepper, onion, and mushrooms; cook till tender. Blend in pimiento, shallots, and flour. Add cream and simmer 5 minutes, stirring constantly. Stir in salt, pepper, dry mustard, Worcestershire sauce, crab meat, and *2 cups* bread crumbs (mixture will be thick). Form into 8 balls. Roll balls in remaining crumbs; place in 8 individual baking dishes. Bake at 350° for 15 to 20 minutes. Remove from oven; top each with 2 tablespoons hollandaise sauce. Brown under broiler for about 1 minute. Serve hot. Makes 8 servings.

Crab-Stuffed Mushrooms

3 dozen large, whole, fresh mushrooms
1 7½-ounce can crab meat, drained, flaked, and cartilage removed
1 tablespoon snipped parsley
1 tablespoon chopped pimiento
1 teaspoon chopped capers

• • •

¼ teaspoon dry mustard
½ cup mayonnaise or salad dressing

Wash and dry mushrooms. With a sharp knife remove stems from mushrooms. (Save stems for use in another recipe.) Combine crab meat, parsley, pimiento, and capers. Blend dry mustard into mayonnaise, toss with crab mixture. Fill each mushroom crown with about 2 tablespoons crab mixture. Bake at 375° till hot, about 8 to 10 minutes. Makes 36 appetizers.

Crab Meat Newberg

6 tablespoons butter
2 tablespoons all-purpose flour
1½ cups light cream
3 beaten egg yolks

• • •

1 cup flaked, cooked crab meat
3 tablespoons dry white wine
2 tablespoons lemon juice
¼ teaspoon salt
Paprika
Pastry Petal Cups

Melt butter in skillet; blend in flour. Add cream all at once. Cook, stirring constantly, till sauce thickens and bubbles.

Stir small amount of hot mixture into egg yolks; return to hot mixture. Cook, stirring constantly, till thickened. Add crab meat; heat through. Add wine, lemon juice, and salt. Sprinkle with paprika. Serve in Pastry Petal Cups or over toast points. Makes 4 or 5 servings.

Pastry Petal Cups: Make Plain Pastry (See *Pastry*) or use piecrust mix. Roll ⅛ inch thick; cut in 2¼-inch rounds. In each of 5 muffin cups, place one round in bottom and overlap 4 rounds on sides; press together. Prick bottoms and sides with a fork. Bake at 450° for 10 to 12 minutes. Cool. A recipe that calls for 1½ cups flour will make 5 pastry cups.

Crab Sandwich Broil

1 7½-ounce can crab meat, drained, flaked, and cartilage removed
½ cup chopped unpeeled apple
¼ cup chopped celery
½ cup mayonnaise
1 tablespoon lemon juice

• • •

3 hamburger buns, split
3 tablespoons butter or margarine, softened
6 slices sharp process American cheese

Combine first 5 ingredients. Toast buns and spread with butter; top each half with ⅓ cup crab mixture. Broil 4 inches from heat for 3 to 4 minutes. Top each with slice of cheese; broil till cheese is slightly melted, about 1 to 2 minutes. Makes 6 servings.

King Crab Crown

1 envelope unflavored gelatin
3 tablespoons cold water
2 tablespoons mayonnaise or salad dressing

• • •

¼ cup lemon juice
2 tablespoons finely snipped parsley
4 teaspoons finely snipped chives
1 tablespoon prepared mustard
¼ teaspoon salt
Dash pepper
1 7½-ounce can crab meat, drained, flaked, and cartilage removed
1 cup whipping cream
Unpeeled cucumber slices cut ¼ inch thick (optional)
Lemon slices

Soften gelatin in cold water; dissolve over hot water. Stir gelatin into mayonnaise. Blend in lemon juice, parsley, chives, mustard, salt, and pepper. Fold in crab meat. Whip cream; fold into salad. Turn salad into 3½-cup mold. Chill till firm, at least 2 hours. Unmold on chilled platter; garnish with cucumber and lemon slices. Makes 6 servings.

Crab-Artichoke Luncheon Salad

Salad greens, torn in bite-sized pieces (6 cups)
1½ pounds frozen king crab legs, thawed and shelled, *or* 1 6-ounce package frozen crab meat, thawed, *or* 1 7½-ounce can crab meat, drained, and cartilage removed
1 9-ounce package frozen artichoke hearts, cooked, drained, and chilled
2 hard-cooked eggs, chopped
Creamy Salad Dressing

In salad bowl, combine greens. Top with crab meat, artichokes, and eggs. Just before serving toss with dressing. Serves 4 to 6.

Creamy Salad Dressing: Whip ½ cup whipping cream. Combine whipped cream, 1 cup mayonnaise, ¼ cup catsup *or* chili sauce, 2 teaspoons lemon juice, and salt to taste. Chill.

Crab-Tomato Aspic

Soften 2 envelopes unflavored gelatin in ½ cup condensed beef broth. Combine 3 cups tomato juice, 2 slices onion, 2 bay leaves, and ¼ teaspoon celery salt; bring to boiling. Remove onion and bay leaves. Add softened gelatin; stir till dissolved. Add ½ cup condensed beef broth and 2 tablespoons lemon juice. Chill mixture till partially set.

Fold 1 cup chopped celery and one 7½-ounce can crab meat, drained, flaked, and cartilage removed, into gelatin mixture. Turn into 5½-cup mold; chill till firm. Unmold; garnish with hard cooked egg wedges and lettuce in center and around sides of mold. Serves 6.

Crack king crab legs and pick out the sweet, white meat for use in cocktails and salads, such as Crab-Artichoke Luncheon Salad.

Garnishing meats with crab apples or apple rings gives a spicy, apple flavor plus a bright, colorful accent to the whole meal.

CRAB APPLE—A small, exceptionally tart variety of apple. These apples are 1½ inches in diameter and red in color. A crab apple yields 70 calories but any syrup added will increase the count.

Fresh crab apples are available in the fall, while canned crab apples can be purchased throughout the year. Those in cans or jars are usually packed in a spicy syrup with the stems still attached for a more attractive appearance.

Use crab apples for making jelly, preserves, sauces, and relishes or for an accompaniment with meat. (See also *Apple*.)

Crab Apple Glaze

Colorful glaze and garnish—

Drain one 27-ounce jar spiced whole crab apples, reserving ½ cup syrup. Combine reserved syrup and 1 cup brown sugar in small saucepan; heat and stir till boiling.

Brush syrup glaze on each side of ham slice during last few minutes of boiling. *Or,* brush on broiler-fryer chicken halves several times during last 10 to 15 minutes of broiling. Add crab apples to remaining syrup in saucepan and heat through. Pass warm crab apples with meat or arrange on serving platter.

CRAB BOIL—A blend of spices also called shrimp spice. (See also *Shrimp Spice.*)

CRAB LOUIS—An elaborate main-dish salad. It consists of a bed of lettuce, lumps of crab meat, wedges of hard-cooked eggs, ripe olives, and tomato quarters. A Louis dressing made of mayonnaise, chili sauce, and lemon tops the salad.

This salad was supposedly created on the Pacific coast in 1914 and has been enjoyed throughout the country ever since.

Crab Louis

Substitute shrimp or lobster for a variation—

4 Bibb lettuce cups
8 cups shredded lettuce (1 large head)
2 to 3 cups cooked crab meat *or* 2 7½-ounce cans crab meat, chilled and drained

• • •

2 large tomatoes, cut in wedges
2 hard-cooked eggs, sliced
Louis Dressing
Pitted ripe olives

Line 4 salad plates with Bibb lettuce cups. Place shredded lettuce atop cups. If necessary, remove cartilage from crab meat. Reserve claw meat; leave remainder in chunks and arrange atop shredded lettuce.

Circle meat with tomato and egg. Sprinkle with salt. Top with claw meat. Pour ¼ *cup* Louis Dressing atop each salad. Garnish with pitted ripe olives. Pass remaining dressing. Makes 4 servings.

Louis Dressing: Whip ¼ cup whipping cream. Fold 1 cup mayonnaise or salad dressing, ¼ cup chili sauce, ¼ cup chopped green pepper, 2 tablespoons sliced green onion with tops, and 1 teaspoon lemon juice into the whipped cream. Season to taste with salt and pepper; chill.

Salad royalty

Crab Louis, a combination of delicate crab meat and tangy dressing, served with breadsticks makes a spectacular luncheon menu. →

CRACKER—A thin, dry, crisp baked product available in a wide range of sizes and shapes as well as an assortment of flavors. In England, crackers are known as biscuits even though baking powder biscuits also retain this same name.

The simplest cracker recipes are a mixture of flour, water or milk, salt, and usually a leavener such as baking powder. Butter is often added to produce a less crumbly product. The dough is rolled thin, cut, and baked till dry and crisp.

Most of the crackers available in the United States are baked commercially. An increasing array of shapes—square, round, oblong, or fancy—and flavors—plain, salted, seeded, seasoned, sweetened, or unsweetened—line the grocery shelves. There's at least one kind of cracker to please every taste.

The manufactured crackers are carefully packaged to ensure crispness. So that this freshness will be retained, be sure to open each package carefully. Unfold the inner wrap so it can be refolded, thus keeping out atmospheric moisture. If the package is accidentally torn, store the crackers in an airtight container.

However, crackers that become limp need not be thrown away. Crisping is easily achieved by spreading the crackers on a cookie sheet and heating them for a few minutes in a slow oven.

Varieties of crackers enhance menus and function as cooking agents, too. Either a single type or an assortment of the unsweetened varieties are excellent for appetizer or in-between-meal nibblers accompanied by dips, dunks, or cheeses. Their compatibility with salads and soups has long been recognized. Sweetened crackers such as graham crackers are favorites with children and adults alike for desserts or snacks. Some dessert crackers are even chocolate-coated for added richness.

Crackers, when used for cooking, are usually crushed or crumbled. One of the main uses of cracker crumbs is as an extender for meat dishes. When used in this way, the dish will yield more servings per pound of meat. At the same time, the flavor and texture from the crackers also will affect that of the final product to which they may be added.

Meat Loaf Supreme

1 pound ground pork
1 pound ground beef
1 cup shredded carrot
1 cup coarsely crushed saltine crackers (22 crackers)
1 cup dairy sour cream
1/4 cup chopped onion
Mushroom Sauce

Combine first 6 ingredients, 1 teaspoon salt, and dash pepper; mix. Press into 9x5x3-inch loaf pan. Bake at 350° about 1 1/2 hours. Let stand 10 minutes; remove from pan. Serve with *Mushroom Sauce:* Dissolve 1 beef bouillon cube, crushed, in drippings from meat loaf. Combine with 1/2 cup dairy sour cream, 1 tablespoon all-purpose flour, and one 3-ounce can broiled sliced mushrooms, undrained. Heat just to boiling. Makes 8 to 10 servings.

Crumbs made from crackers may serve to bind ingredients together or to thicken a mixture. They are frequently used in casseroles for such purposes. Soups and sauces can be thickened in this manner.

Salmon Scallop

1 7 3/4-ounce can salmon, undrained
1/2 cup finely crushed saltine crackers (14 crackers)
1/3 cup milk
1/4 cup chopped celery
2 teaspoons lemon juice
Dash dried dillweed
1 tablespoon butter or margarine

Flake salmon with liquid in bowl, removing skin and bones. Stir in dash pepper and remaining ingredients *except* butter. Turn into 1/2-quart casserole. Dot with butter. Bake at 350° for 35 minutes. Makes 2 servings.

Cracker-crumb piecrusts make versatile variations for main dishes or desserts. If the crust is baked before adding the filling, the resulting piecrust will be a little crisper. Unbaked dessert crumb crusts should be chilled, then filled.

Ham in Cheese Crust

1½ cups finely crushed round cheese crackers (about 36)
6 tablespoons butter or margarine, melted

• • •

2 beaten eggs
1 6-ounce can evaporated milk (⅔ cup)
¼ cup finely chopped onion
¼ cup finely chopped green pepper
1 tablespoon prepared mustard
1 teaspoon prepared horseradish
1 pound ground fully cooked ham

For crust mix cracker crumbs and butter. Reserving 2 tablespoons crumb mixture, press remaining on bottom and sides of 9-inch pie plate. Bake at 350° for 10 minutes.

Meanwhile, in a bowl combine eggs, evaporated milk, chopped onion, chopped green pepper, mustard, and horseradish. Add ham; mix well. Turn into baked crumb crust. Bake at 350° for 35 minutes.

Sprinkle with reserved 2 tablespoons crumb mixture; bake 5 to 10 minutes longer. Let stand 5 minutes before cutting into wedges. If desired, trim top of pie with additional whole round cheese crackers and a few sprigs of fresh parsley. Makes 6 servings.

Cheese cracker crumbs not only form the shell for Ham in Cheese Crust, but they add an attractive garnish to the top. Additional crackers and parsley are added before serving.

S'More Pie

- 1¼ cups finely crushed graham crackers
- ¼ cup sugar
- 6 tablespoons butter or margarine, melted
- 2 cups milk
- 2 slightly beaten egg yolks
- 1 3- or 3¼-ounce package *regular* vanilla pudding mix
- 1 cup miniature marshmallows
- 3 ¾-ounce milk chocolate candy bars, broken in pieces
- 2 egg whites
- ½ teaspoon vanilla
- ¼ teaspoon cream of tartar
- ¼ cup sugar

Combine crumbs, the first ¼ cup sugar, and melted butter; mix well. Press firmly on bottom and sides of 9-inch pie plate. Bake at 375° till edges are brown, about 6 to 8 minutes; cool.

Combine milk and egg yolks; gradually add to pudding mix in saucepan. Cook according to package directions. Cover surface of pudding with waxed paper; cool.

Place marshmallows over crust; top with chocolate pieces. Spoon cooled pudding evenly over chocolate. Beat egg whites with vanilla and cream of tartar till soft peaks form. Gradually add ¼ cup sugar, beating to stiff peaks. Spread atop pie, sealing to edges of crust. Bake at 375° till golden, about 10 to 12 minutes. Cool thoroughly before serving.

Assorted crackers, attractively arranged, make the ideal partner with Chicken Liver-Onion Dip. (See *Dip* for recipe.)

Crackers, whole or crushed, also make an attractive and appealing garnish. On casseroles, crumbs may be added just before baking. Garnish desserts with whole or crushed crackers before serving.

Make cracker crumbs in blender

Use your blender to make cracker crumbs in a hurry. Turn blender on and off quickly to regulate desired fineness of crumbs.

Saltine crackers—to make ½ cup of cracker crumbs, place 13 to 14 crackers in blender container. These can be done all at the same time.

Graham crackers—To make ½ cup of Graham cracker crumbs, break 6 to 7 crackers into the blender container.

Oven-Style Turkey Hash

- 1½ cups coarsely ground cooked turkey
- 1 cup cubed cooked potato
- 1 6-ounce can evaporated milk
- ¼ cup finely snipped parsley
- ¼ cup finely chopped onion
- 1 teaspoon Worcestershire sauce
- ½ teaspoon salt
- ¼ teaspoon ground sage

• • •

- ¼ cup finely crushed saltine crackers (7 crackers)
- 1 tablespoon butter, melted

Stir together first 8 ingredients and dash pepper. Turn into lightly greased 1-quart casserole. Toss crumbs and butter together. Sprinkle atop hash. Bake, uncovered, at 350° till heated through, about 30 minutes. Makes 4 servings.

Mushroom Casserole

Serve as a meat accompaniment or over toast for a main dish—

Cook ½ cup chopped onion in ½ cup butter or margarine till crisp-tender. Add two 6-ounce cans mushroom crowns, drained. Cook lightly. Blend in ¼ cup all-purpose flour and ½ teaspoon dried marjoram leaves, crushed. Add one 10½-ounce can condensed beef broth all at once. Cook and stir till mixture is thickened and bubbly. Remove from heat. Stir in 2 tablespoons dry sherry and 2 tablespoons snipped parsley. Pour mixture into 1-quart casserole.

Combine ½ cup coarsely crushed saltine crackers (11 crackers), 2 tablespoons grated Parmesan cheese, and 1 tablespoon melted butter or margarine. Sprinkle over top of casserole. Bake at 375° till mixture is hot and bubbly, about 15 minutes. Makes 6 servings.

Crush crackers the easy way with a pizza roller, glass, or rolling pin. The plastic bag, fastened securely, corrals the crumbs.

As an outside coating, cracker crumbs add an interesting texture and flavor. Try coating fried and baked foods, such as meatballs, croquettes, chicken, or vegetables with crumbs. A double dipping, of course, gives more crunch. Crumbs also make an equally delicious stuffing.

Cracker Stuffing

1 cup chopped celery
¾ cup chopped onion
¼ cup butter or margarine
2 cups coarsely crushed saltine crackers (44 crackers)
¾ cup milk
1 slightly beaten egg
1 tablespoon snipped parsley
1 teaspoon dried sage leaves, crushed
¼ teaspoon dried thyme leaves, crushed
½ teaspoon salt

In medium skillet cook celery and onion in butter till tender but not brown. Moisten crackers with milk; add onion mixture, egg, parsley, dried sage, dried thyme, salt, and dash pepper. Makes 2⅔ cups stuffing or enough to stuff one 3- to 4-pound chicken.

Sesame Chicken

⅔ cup finely crushed saltine crackers (18 crackers)
¼ cup sesame seed, toasted
1 2½- to 3-pound ready-to-cook broiler-fryer chicken, cut up
½ 6-ounce can evaporated milk (⅓ cup)
½ cup butter, melted

Combine crumbs and toasted sesame seed. Dip chicken pieces in evaporated milk, then roll in crumb mixture. Pour melted butter into 11¾x7½x1¾-inch baking dish. Dip skin side of chicken pieces in butter; turn over and arrange, skin side up, in baking dish. Bake, uncovered, at 375° till done, about 1 hour. Makes 4 servings.

CRACKER MEAL—The commercial name for fine, unsweetened cracker crumbs.

CRACKLING—1. A crisp bit of tissue that remains after fresh pork fat has been rendered into lard. It is especially liked by Southerners. 2. The crunchy, well-browned fat on roast pork.

CRACKLING BREAD—A corn bread in which crisp cracklings are used as shortening.

CRANBERRY—Bright, red, acid berry of several trailing plants of the heath family. The fruit, native to North America—from Newfoundland to North Carolina and as far west as the states of Minnesota and Arkansas—thrives in cool regions of the Northern Hemisphere. The cultivated berries which have also been introduced into Washington, Oregon, and British Columbia are large, ranging in size from ⅓ to ¾ inch in diameter. (The highbush cranberry, is not a member of this botanical family.)

Species different from those in North America are found in parts of the world with similar climates. The European varieties, however, are somewhat smaller in size with berries from ¼ to ⅓ inch in diameter. One of the better-known species is the lingonberry grown in Scandinavia.

Among the first gifts brought to the Pilgrims by friendly Indians were wild cranberries native to the Massachusetts countryside. Besides eating the berries, the Indians used the brightly colored cranberry juice to dye rugs and blankets and the crushed fruit in a poultice.

The name cranberry is a variation of craneberry, given to the fruit because the pale pink blossoms resemble the head of a crane. In addition, cranes were seen enjoying the fruit while wading in the bogs where cranberries grow.

Cultivation of cranberries did not begin until some 200 years after the landing of the Pilgrims in the New World. A very alert New Englander noted that the largest and juiciest berries were on vines covered by sand blown in from the seashore. Thirty years after this observation the first cranberry bog was built—it is still producing berries. Today, cranberries are grown commercially not only in Massachusetts, but also in New Jersey, Wisconsin, Washington, and Oregon. A limited number of cranberries are also grown in Rhode Island, Michigan, and Maine.

Winter salad bowl spectacular

← Cubes of canned cranberry sauce and tiny orange sections glisten amongst crisp greens in a colorful Cran-Mandarin Toss.

Commercially grown cranberries grow on peat soil that has been covered with a layer of sand. The vines are weeded in the spring and pruned in the fall. Re-sanding is necessary every three to four years. Cranberries are picked and marketed in the fall, a season when an early frost is a definite hazard. Weather forecasts are carefully heeded. When there is the prospect of frost, the vines are protected from frost by flooding the bogs.

In the early days, cranberries were picked by hand. Next came the wooden fingered scoops which combed the berries from the vines. Now mechanical pickers have taken over the job, doing the harvesting in a shorter time. There is even a type of water harvesting in which the berries are knocked off the vines onto flooded fields and floated onto conveyers.

Nutritional value: Raw cranberries are relatively low in calories. One cup of berries contains 46 calories, but this increases as sugar or other ingredients are added to temper the natural sourness of the fruit. Thus, one-half cup cranberry sauce prepared at home will contain approximately 178 calories. Cranberries are also sources of iron and vitamin C.

Fresh cranberries: Good quality in fresh berries is indicated by fresh, plump appearance with a high luster and firmness of fruit. The shade of red does not indicate ripeness because each variety of cranberry produces fruit with a slightly different red hue—some light, some dark.

Good berries bounce when dropped; poor berries just roll. Thus, bounce is one of the tests fresh cranberries must pass when being sorted and graded for market or for use by a processor. The homemaker in her kitchen washing cranberries for use in a recipe will also discard berries that are soft or have bruises.

Cranberries are marketed in several forms. During the fall months the berries are available fresh. At other times whole berries may be found in frozen food cases. All year round shoppers will see canned and frozen cranberry products such as sauce, relish, and juice cocktail, packaged alone or in combination with other fruits.

Fresh cranberries lend their cheery color and tart flavor to many dishes. There are tempting relishes to accompany meat and poultry plus fragrant breads, salads, and easy, colorful desserts.

Cranberry Sauce

Use this same basic recipe to prepare either a spoonable sauce or one to serve jellied—

2 cups sugar
2 cups water
1 pound fresh cranberries (4 cups)

Combine sugar and water in large saucepan; stir to dissolve sugar. Heat to boiling; boil 5 minutes. Add cranberries; cook till skins pop, about 5 minutes. Remove from heat. Serve warm or chilled. Makes 4 cups.

To mold, cook longer till a drop jells on cold plate, about 10 minutes. Pour into 4½-cup mold. Chill till firm.

Pass Cranberry-Date Relish, a medley of fruits, nuts, and spices, especially created for enjoyment with the holiday bird.

Celery Cran-Relish

An uncooked accompaniment, sweet yet tangy—

1 pound fresh cranberries (4 cups)
2 cups coarsely chopped celery
1 medium unpeeled apple, cut up
1½ cups sugar
2 tablespoons lemon juice

Using coarse blade of food chopper, grind the cranberries, celery, and apple. Stir in sugar and lemon juice; chill. Will keep in refrigerator for several weeks. Makes about 4 cups.

Cranberry-Date Relish

Cooked relish that takes only minutes to prepare—

1 pound fresh cranberries (4 cups)
1 cup sugar
1 cup snipped dates
½ cup light raisins
2 cups water
¼ cup vinegar
¼ teaspoon ground cinnamon
¼ teaspoon ground ginger

In a medium saucepan combine cranberries, sugar, snipped dates, raisins, water, vinegar, cinnamon, and ginger. Bring to boiling point and boil rapidly, uncovered, for about 10 minutes, stirring occasionally. Remove from heat. Chill. Makes 4 cups relish.

Cranberry Waldorf

2 cups fresh cranberries
3 cups miniature marshmallows
¾ cup sugar
2 cups diced unpeeled tart apple
½ cup seedless green grapes
½ cup broken walnuts
¼ teaspoon salt
1 cup whipping cream

Grind cranberries and combine with marshmallows and sugar. Cover and chill overnight. Add apple, grapes, walnuts, and salt. Whip cream; fold into fruits. Chill. Serve in a large bowl or in individual lettuce cups. Garnish with grapes, if desired. Serves 8 to 10.

Tantalize guests by serving Cranberry Ice when the turkey is being carved. This pretty pink accompaniment is not dessert. Instead, its a refreshing treat with meat or poultry.

Cranberry-Banana Bread

Cream ¼ cup butter and 1 cup sugar. Add 1 egg; beat. Sift 2 cups sifted all-purpose flour, 3 teaspoons baking powder, and ½ teaspoon *each* salt and ground cinnamon. Add alternately with mixture of 1 cup mashed banana, ¼ cup milk, and 1 teaspoon shredded orange peel. Stir in 1½ cups fresh cranberries, ground and drained, and 1 cup chopped pecans. Turn into greased 9x5x3-inch pan; bake at 350° 1 hour.

Cranberry Coleslaw

Combine ¼ cup sliced fresh cranberries, 1 tablespoon honey, and 1 teaspoon celery seed; let stand 15 minutes. Add ¼ cup mayonnaise and 1 teaspoon vinegar; mix. Toss with 3 cups shredded cabbage. Season. Serves 4 to 5.

Cranberry Nut Loaf

Bright flecks of cranberry in every slice—

3 cups sifted all-purpose flour
1 cup sugar
4 teaspoons baking powder
1 teaspoon salt
1 beaten egg
1½ cups milk
2 tablespoons salad oil
1 cup coarsely chopped cranberries
½ cup chopped nuts

Sift together dry ingredients. Combine egg, milk, and salad oil; add to dry ingredients, stirring just till moistened. Stir in cranberries and nuts. Turn mixture into greased 9x5x3-inch loaf pan. Bake at 350° till done, about 1¼ hours. Remove from pan; cool on rack.

Cranberry Chutney

1 pound fresh cranberries (4 cups)
2¼ cups brown sugar
1 cup light raisins
½ cup coarsely chopped macadamia nuts *or* toasted almonds
¼ cup snipped candied ginger
¼ cup lemon juice
2 teaspoons salt
1 teaspoon grated onion
¼ teaspoon ground cloves

In large saucepan combine all ingredients with 1 cup water. Bring to boiling, stirring constantly. Simmer, uncovered, over low heat for 15 minutes, stirring occasionally. Pack in hot scalded jars; seal at once and refrigerate till used. Makes about 5 half pints.

Cranberry-Banana Shortcake

A fruit duet topping tender, rich desserts—

1 cup sugar
2 cups fresh cranberries
2 bananas, sliced
6 individual biscuits *or* short cakes (see *Biscuit*)

Combine sugar and ½ cup water in saucepan and stir until dissolved. Boil 5 minutes. Add cranberries and cook till skins pop, about 5 minutes. Remove from heat. Stir in banana slices. Serve on biscuits. Top with whipped cream, if desired. Makes 6 servings.

Cranberry-Avocado Mold

2 3-ounce packages raspberry-flavored gelatin
2 cups boiling water
1 cup fresh cranberries, ground
½ cup sugar
1 avocado, peeled and cubed
¼ cup chopped walnuts

Dissolve gelatin in boiling water; add 1½ cups cold water. Chill till partially set. Combine cranberries, sugar, dash salt, avocado, and nuts; fold into gelatin. Pour into 6½-cup mold; chill till firm. Makes 8 servings.

Cranberry juice cocktail: Its sparkling, clear red color and not-too-sweet flavor make this bottled fruit drink popular as a breakfast beverage or served as an appetizer for a change of pace. The juice is sweetened and vitamin C is usually added during processing. A 5-ounce serving contains about 65 calories.

Because it mixes well with other fruit juices or carbonated beverages, cranberry juice cocktail is an excellent base for fruit punch or mixed drinks served over ice. It may also be used to make a beautiful jelly or to provide the liquid in a glowing molded salad filled with fruit.

Cranberry Jelly

A clear, ruby-red jelly to give away or enjoy at the family holiday feast—

3½ cups cranberry juice cocktail
1 2¼-ounce package powdered fruit pectin
4 cups sugar
¼ cup lemon juice

In large saucepan or kettle, combine cranberry juice and pectin. Stir over high heat till cranberry mixture comes to full rolling boil. Stir in sugar immediately. Bring to full rolling boil again; boil hard 2 minutes, stirring constantly. Remove from heat; stir in lemon juice. Skim foam off surface. Pour jelly into hot scalded jars. Makes 6 half pints.

Cranberry-Waldorf Mold

2 cups cranberry juice cocktail
1 3-ounce package lemon-flavored gelatin

. . .

¼ teaspoon salt
1 cup diced unpeeled apple
½ cup chopped celery
¼ cup broken walnuts

Heat *1 cup* cranberry juice cocktail and gelatin over low heat till gelatin is dissolved. Add remaining juice and the salt. Chill till partially set. Stir in apple, celery, and nuts. Pour into 4 to 6 individual molds. Chill firm. Serves 4 to 6.

Cranberry-Tea Punch

5 tea bags *or* 5 teaspoons loose tea
¼ teaspoon ground cinnamon
¼ teaspoon ground nutmeg
¾ cup sugar
2 cups cranberry juice cocktail
½ cup orange juice
⅓ cup lemon juice

Steep tea and spices in 2½ cups boiling water 5 minutes. Remove tea. Add sugar; stir till dissolved; cool. Add fruit juices and 1½ cups water. Chill. Serve over ice. Serves 6 to 8.

Ruby Fruit Punch

1 28-ounce bottle ginger ale, chilled
1 tablespoon lemon juice
Orange slices
4 cups cranberry juice cocktail, chilled
1 cup apple juice, chilled

Place chilled ginger ale, lemon juice, and a few orange slices in punch bowl. Slowly add chilled cranberry juice cocktail and chilled apple juice, stirring gently to blend. Add ice cubes. Makes about 16 servings.

Gaily-bobbing orange slices decorate the punch bowl brimming with Ruby Fruit Punch. Another time serve a tea-based cranberry party punch delicately spiced with cinnamon.

Canned jellied and whole cranberry sauce: Although most often spooned right from the can to the serving dish, these handy sauces are very useful as an ingredient. They are used as basting sauces for hamburgers and pot roasts. Spicy beverages, tossed and molded salads, quick breads, such as muffins, and desserts depend upon these sauces for flavor and color.

Cranberry Ice

A sophisticated partner for the holiday turkey—

1 16-ounce can jellied cranberry sauce
1 7-ounce bottle lemon-lime carbonated beverage

Beat cranberry sauce till smooth. Resting bottom on rim of bowl, slowly pour in lemon-lime beverage. Mix gently with up-and-down motion. Pour mixture into 1-quart freezer tray. Freeze till firm. Break into chunks with wooden spoon and place in chilled bowl. Beat till fluffy. Return mixture to freezer tray and freeze till firm. Makes 1 quart.

Hot Buttered Cranberry Swizzle

3/4 cup brown sugar
1 cup water
1/2 teaspoon ground cinnamon
1/2 teaspoon ground allspice
1/2 teaspoon ground cloves
1/4 teaspoon salt
1/4 teaspoon ground nutmeg
2 16-ounce cans jellied cranberry sauce
3 cups water
4 cups pineapple juice
Butter or margarine
Cinnamon sticks

In large saucepan combine brown sugar, the 1 cup water, the ground cinnamon, allspice, cloves, salt, and nutmeg. Cook over medium heat till boiling. Add cranberry sauce and beat till smooth. Slowly stir in the 3 cups water. Add pineapple juice; simmer, uncovered, about 5 minutes. Serve in mugs. Dot with butter. Serve with cinnamon sticks. Serves 10 to 12.

Chicken Pecan Salad in Shimmering Cranberry Ring

2 3-ounce packages lemon-flavored gelatin
1/4 teaspoon salt
2 cups orange juice
1 16-ounce can whole cranberry sauce
3 medium peaches, peeled and sliced (1 1/2 cups)*
3 cups cubed cooked chicken
1 cup diced celery

• • •

1/2 cup mayonnaise
2 tablespoons salad oil
1 tablespoon vinegar
1/2 teaspoon salt
1/4 cup toasted broken pecans

Dissolve gelatin and salt in *1 cup* orange juice and 1 cup water, heated to boiling. Stir in 1 cup cold orange juice. Chill till partially set. Stir in whole cranberry sauce. Pour into 6 1/2-cup ring mold. Chill till firm.

Reserve a few peach slices for garnish. Cut up remaining peaches. In large bowl, combine cut up peaches, chicken, and celery. Blend together mayonnaise, salad oil, vinegar, and salt. Toss with chicken mixture. Chill. Before serving, fold in nuts. Serve in center of Cranberry Ring. Garnish with peaches. Makes 6 servings.
*To keep bright color, dip in lemon or orange juice mixed with a little water.

Cranberry-Apricot Salad

1 16-ounce jar refrigerated fruit salad
1 16-ounce can jellied cranberry sauce, chilled
1 cup seedless green grapes
1 22-ounce can apricot pie filling
1 cup miniature marshmallows
1/2 cup chopped pecans

Drain fruit salad thoroughly. Cut cranberry sauce into 1/2-inch cubes and add to fruit salad. Fold in grapes, apricot pie filling, and marshmallows. Chill salad mixture thoroughly, about 4 to 5 hours. Just before serving, stir in the chopped pecans. Makes 6 to 8 servings.

Cranberry Star Mold practically makes itself when canned whole cranberry sauce and crushed pineapple team up in a do-ahead salad. The garnish is orange and grapefruit sections.

Cranberry Star Mold

2 3-ounce packages orange-flavored gelatin
1 16-ounce can whole cranberry sauce
1 8¾-ounce can crushed pineapple, undrained
2 7-ounce bottles ginger ale
Canned orange and grapefruit sections

In saucepan combine gelatin and cranberry sauce. Heat and stir till almost boiling and gelatin is dissolved. Stir in undrained pineapple and ginger ale. When fizzing has stopped, pour into 5½-cup star mold. Chill till set. Unmold.

Garnish with greens and orange and grapefruit sections. If desired, center sections with a few whole cranberries. Serve with mayonnaise or salad dressing. Makes 8 servings.

Cran-Cheese Frosties

1 16-ounce can jellied cranberry sauce
2 tablespoons lemon juice
1 3-ounce package cream cheese, softened
¼ cup mayonnaise or salad dressing
¼ cup sifted confectioners' sugar
¼ cup chopped walnuts
1 cup whipping cream

Beat cranberry sauce and lemon juice till smooth. Pour into 6 to 8 paper baking cups, filling about ⅓ full *or* one 4-cup freezer tray. Beat together softened cream cheese, mayonnaise, and confectioners' sugar. Stir in walnuts. Whip cream. Fold whipped cream into cream cheese mixture; spread over cranberry layer. Freeze till firm. Serve on lettuce. Serves 6 to 8.

Cran-Mandarin Toss

1 envelope creamy French salad dressing mix
½ teaspoon grated orange peel
8 cups torn mixed salad greens
1 11-ounce can mandarin orange sections, drained
1 8-ounce can jellied cranberry sauce, chilled and cubed

Prepare salad dressing mix according to package directions, adding orange peel; chill. In large salad bowl toss together greens and mandarin orange sections. Add cranberry sauce cubes to salad and mix gently. Spoon onto salad plates. Pass dressing. Makes 8 servings.

Cranberry Burger Sauce

1 16-ounce can whole cranberry sauce
¼ cup finely chopped celery
1 tablespoon brown sugar
3 tablespoons Worcestershire sauce
1 tablespoon salad oil

Combine all ingredients. Grill hamburgers a few minutes on each side before basting with sauce. Makes about 2 cups sauce.

Cranberry-Raisin Stuffing

14 cups soft bread cubes (about 14 slices bread)
¼ cup butter or margarine, melted
1 16-ounce can whole cranberry sauce
½ cup raisins
¼ cup sugar
1 teaspoon salt
1 teaspoon lemon juice
½ teaspoon ground cinnamon

Toast bread cubes in 300° oven for about 15 minutes; toss with melted butter or margarine. Add cranberry sauce, raisins, sugar, salt, lemon juice, and cinnamon; toss lightly till well mixed. Makes 8 cups stuffing. This amount is enough to stuff a 12-pound turkey.

Cranberry Pot Roast

2 tablespoons all-purpose flour
1 teaspoon salt
1 teaspoon onion salt
¼ teaspoon pepper
1 3- to 4-pound round-bone pot roast
2 tablespoons salad oil
4 whole cloves
2 inches stick cinnamon
¼ cup water
1 16-ounce can whole cranberry sauce
1 tablespoon vinegar

Combine flour, salt, onion salt, and pepper; rub onto surfaces of meat (use all of mixture). In Dutch oven slowly brown meat on both sides in oil. Add spices and water. Cover tightly; simmer till tender, about 2½ hours. Add more water if necessary.

Pour off excess fat. To meat add cranberry sauce, 2 tablespoons water, and vinegar; cover and cook 10 to 15 minutes. Pass sauce with meat. Makes 6 to 8 servings.

Plymouth Cranberry Cake

1 16-ounce can whole cranberry sauce
2 tablespoons butter or margarine
1 package 1-layer-size white cake mix
¼ cup butter or margarine
½ cup sifted confectioners' sugar
½ cup cold water
1½ *teaspoons* cornstarch
1 teaspoon vanilla
½ teaspoon vinegar

Break up cranberry sauce in buttered 8¼x1¾-inch round ovenware cake dish, spreading evenly. Dot with 2 tablespoons butter. Prepare cake mix according to package directions; pour over cranberries. Bake at 350° for 35 to 40 minutes. Let stand 10 minutes; invert on plate. Serve warm with *Butter Sauce:* Cream ¼ cup butter. Gradually add confectioners' sugar, creaming till fluffy. In small saucepan, combine cold water and cornstarch; cook and stir till thick and bubbly. Stir into butter mixture. Add vanilla and vinegar. Serve warm.

Cranberry Cheese Pie

1⅓ cups flaked coconut
¼ cup melted butter or margarine
1 8-ounce package cream cheese
½ cup whipping cream
¼ cup sugar
½ teaspoon vanilla
1 16-ounce can whole cranberry sauce

Toast coconut in a 350° oven about 10 minutes, stirring often. Combine with butter or margarine. Press into an 8-inch pie plate.

Beat cream cheese till softened. Whip cream till thickened, but not stiff; add sugar and vanilla. Gradually add to cream cheese beating till smooth and creamy. Fold in cranberry sauce. Spoon into crust. Chill until firm.

Cranberry-Cube Muffins

1 8-ounce can jellied cranberry sauce
1¾ cups sifted all-purpose flour
¼ cup sugar
2½ teaspoons baking powder
¾ teaspoon salt
1 well-beaten egg
¾ cup milk
⅓ cup salad oil

Cut cranberry sauce into ½-inch cubes; set aside. Sift flour, sugar, baking powder, and salt into a bowl. Make a well in the center. Combine egg, milk, and oil. Add all at once to dry ingredients. Stir quickly, just till dry ingredients are moistened. Fill greased muffin cups ⅓ full. Sprinkle cranberry cubes over batter. Add more batter till muffin cups are ⅔ full. Bake muffins at 400° for about 25 minutes. Makes 12 muffins.

Other cranberry products: The shopper will find cranberries appearing as an ingredient in packaged mixes for quick breads or in a tasty canned or frozen relish to serve with meat and poultry. Cranberry-orange relish is particularly handy to use in perking up a molded gelatin salad or to top canned peach halves as a quick meat accompaniment. (See also *Berry.*)

Cranberry Relish Salad

Thaw one 10-ounce package frozen cranberry-orange relish. Dissolve one 3-ounce package strawberry-flavored gelatin in 1 cup boiling water. Drain one 8¾-ounce can pineapple tidbits reserving the syrup. Add enough water to the syrup to measure ½ cup. Add syrup and relish to gelatin. Chill till partially set. Stir in pineapple and ⅓ cup finely chopped celery. Chill in 4½-cup mold till firm. Serves 6.

CRAPPIE—A freshwater member of the sunfish family, native only to the United States. They are found in Eastern and Midwestern ponds, creeks, lakes, and rivers, especially in the Great Lakes region and the Mississippi River. Both white and black crappies are prized by the sports fisherman because these fish are aggressive fighters even though their average size is only 10 to 12 inches in length.

The flesh of the crappie is tender, white, and flavorful. These fish are excellent for panfrying. (See also *Fish.*)

CRAWDAD—A colloquial name in the United States for crayfish or crawfish.

CRAYFISH, CRAWFISH—Several varieties of shellfish which resemble the lobster but are only distantly related to it. The larger varieties, also known as spiny lobster and rock lobster, are found in Atlantic waters off the southern coast of the United States and in the Caribbean area. Similar types, some growing very large, are found in the Mediterranean and western Pacific.

The small American crayfish is found in fresh water in the Midwest and Pacific states, in particular. The flavor of all varieties resembles that of lobster, and the meat can be used just as lobster would be in sauced dishes. In Sweden boiled crayfish is a popular dish. The French prepare it in a bisque, in a delicious cold mousse, or serve it *au gratin. (See Lobster, Shellfish* for additional information.)

CRAZY PUDDING—A name given to pudding cakes which look like cake batter when they go into the oven, but create a sauce during baking. (See also *Pudding Cake.*)

CREAM ***(noun)***—The fat-rich portion which rises to the top when milk has not been homogenized. This is quite easy to skim off by hand or with a mechanical separator because cream is lighter in weight than milk. The separator removes the cream by centrifugal force and can be adjusted so that cream of any given fat content is produced. The cream is then removed, pasteurized, and may be homogenized.

Cream should always be stored in the refrigerator. Used alone or as a recipe ingredient, cream provides calories and a small amount of vitamin A in the diet.

Calories in cream

The calorie content reflects the percentage of milk fat in the cream. The following table lists the *calories found in 1 tablespoon:*

Half and half (10 to 12% fat)	20
Dairy sour cream (not less than 18% fat)	29
Light cream (not less than 18% fat)	32
Whipping cream	
Light (30 to 36% fat)	45
Heavy (not less than 36% fat)	52

Pasteurized cream whips, sold in pressurized cans, contain added ingredients such as sugar, flavorings, and stabilizers. Other products resembling cream made with non-milk fats and milk solids are also marketed. In addition, dried or frozen cream substitutes containing no dairy products are available on the market.

There are many uses for cream. It adds richness and flavor to beverages, salads, sauces, and desserts. Light cream, often called table or coffee cream, is used for coffee, fruit, and cereal as well as in cooking. Whipped cream provides volume in numerous desserts. It also serves as an attractive garnish. (See *Half and Half, Light Cream, Sour Cream, Whipping Cream* for additional information.)

Sherried Ice Cream Roll

4 egg whites
½ cup granulated sugar
4 egg yolks
¼ cup granulated sugar
½ teaspoon vanilla
⅔ cup sifted cake flour
¼ cup unsweetened cocoa powder
1 teaspoon baking powder
¼ teaspoon salt
Confectioners' sugar
Sherried Ice Cream
Whipped cream

Beat egg whites till soft peaks form; gradually add the ½ cup granulated sugar. Beat till stiff peaks form. Beat egg yolks till thick and lemon colored; gradually beat in the ¼ cup granulated sugar. Add vanilla. Fold yolks into whites. Sift together flour, cocoa, baking powder, and salt; fold into egg mixture.

Spread batter evenly in greased and lightly floured 15½x10½x1-inch jelly roll pan. Bake at 375° till done, about 10 to 12 minutes.

Immediately loosen sides and turn out on towel sprinkled with sifted confectioners' sugar. Starting at narrow end, roll cake and towel together; cool on rack.

To prepare *Sherried Ice Cream:* Combine 2 cups soft coconut macaroon crumbs (9 macaroons) and ¼ cup dry sherry. Stir into 1 quart vanilla ice cream, softened. Add 1 cup dairy sour cream; mix well. Freeze in freezer tray.

To assemble, stir sherried ice cream to soften. Unroll jelly roll and spread with ice cream. Roll up; wrap in foil. Freeze. Garnish with whipped cream. Serves 10 to 12.

Cream-laden desserts

Whether it is ice cream, whipped cream, or → dairy sour cream, cream adds richness to this display of desserts—Sherried Ice Cream Roll, Pineapple Parfait Cake (see *Ice Cream* for recipe), and Party Pumpkin Pie.

Party Pumpkin Pie

1 pint vanilla ice cream, softened
1 tablespoon snipped candied ginger
1 *baked* 9-inch pastry shell, cooled
1 cup canned pumpkin
½ cup sugar
½ teaspoon salt
½ teaspoon ground ginger
¼ teaspoon ground nutmeg
1 cup whipping cream
1½ cups miniature marshmallows

Combine ice cream and candied ginger. Spread in cooled pastry shell. Freeze. Mix pumpkin and next 4 ingredients. Whip cream; fold into pumpkin mixture. Fold in marshmallows. Pile atop ice cream layer; freeze. Garnish with additional whipped cream, if desired.

Gourmet Pork Chops

6 loin pork chops, about ½ inch thick
2 tablespoons all-purpose flour
1 teaspoon salt
Dash pepper
1 10½-ounce can condensed cream of mushroom soup
¾ cup water
½ teaspoon ground ginger
¼ teaspoon dried rosemary leaves, crushed
1 3½-ounce can French-fried onions
½ cup dairy sour cream

Trim excess fat from chops. Heat fat in skillet till about 2 tablespoons melted fat has collected; discard trimmings. Coat chops in mixture of flour, salt, and pepper. Brown in hot fat. Place in 11x7x1½-inch baking pan.

Combine soup, water, ginger, and rosemary; pour over chops. Sprinkle with *half* the onions. Cover; bake at 350° till meat is tender, about 50 minutes. Uncover; sprinkle with remaining onions. Bake, uncovered, 10 minutes more.

Remove meat to platter. Blend sour cream into soup mixture; heat through, *but do not boil.* Pass with meat. Makes 6 servings.

Raspberry Cream Pudding

Thoroughly drain one 10-ounce package frozen raspberries, thawed, reserving syrup. Chill berries. Add water to reserved syrup to make 1½ cups. Combine one 3- or 3¼-ounce package regular vanilla pudding mix with the 1½ cups liquid. Cook and stir over medium heat till mixture comes to boiling. Remove from heat. Cover; chill till thick, about 2 hours.

Beat chilled mixture smooth with rotary beater. Whip ½ cup whipping cream. Fold whipped cream into pudding mixture. Spoon into sherbet glasses; chill about 2 hours.

To serve, wreathe puddings with ¼ cup vanilla wafer crumbs (6 or 7 wafers); top with well-drained raspberries. Makes 4 to 6 servings.

Basic Vanilla Ice Cream

¾ cup sugar
½ envelope unflavored gelatin (1½ teaspoons)
4 cups light cream
1 slightly beaten egg
2 teaspoons vanilla

In saucepan combine sugar and gelatin. Add *2 cups* of the cream. Stir over low heat till gelatin dissolves. Slowly stir small amount of hot mixture into egg; mix well.

Return to hot mixture; cook, stirring constantly, till mixture is slightly thickened, about 1 minute. Remove from heat; chill. Add remaining cream, vanilla, and dash salt. Freeze in ice cream freezer. Makes 1½ quarts.

Strawberry Ice Cream: Prepare Basic Vanilla Ice Cream *except decrease sugar to ½ cup and reduce vanilla to 1 teaspoon.* Crush 4 cups fresh, ripe strawberries; combine with ¾ cup sugar. Stir crushed berries into chilled mixture. Freeze in ice cream freezer.

Peach Ice Cream: Prepare Basic Vanilla Ice Cream *except decrease sugar to ½ cup and reduce vanilla to 1 teaspoon.* Combine 3 cups mashed, fresh peaches; ¾ cup sugar; and ¼ teaspoon almond extract; stir into chilled mixture. Freeze in ice cream freezer.

Cherry Ice Cream: Prepare Basic Vanilla Ice Cream *except reduce vanilla to 1 teaspoon.* To chilled mixture stir in ⅓ cup maraschino cherries, chopped, and 1 tablespoon maraschino cherry juice. Freeze in ice cream freezer.

CREAM ***(verb)***—To beat to a light and fluffy consistency. Shortening may be creamed alone or together with sugar until it is very soft and creamy. A mixture may be creamed by using an electric mixer or by rubbing the mixture against the side of a bowl with the back of a spoon.

CREAM CHEESE—Soft, unripened cheese made from light cream. The origin of cream cheese is unclear. Most likely it originated with early nomadic tribesmen who had to contend with the problem of utilizing soured milk. Having a limited food supply, they were reluctant to discard any food, regardless of its freshness. They learned that milk, like meat, was more easily preserved when dried. So, they developed methods for evaporating milk.

One method devised was to allow fresh milk, poured into shallow containers, to sour under the heat of the sun. As part of the moisture was lost in the process, a thick, acid curd was left. The mixture, similar to what is known as yogurt today, could be further dried to obtain "dried cream"—a primitive form of cream cheese. Another method of evaporating the milk consisted of spooning the curd of soured and separated milk into a wicker mold. The curd was then pressed and drained to remove all the whey.

In time, cream replaced milk in the process. It was allowed to dry in a perforated box lined with two loose layers of cheesecloth. After drying, a firm, but spreadable cheese remained.

Cream cheese, like most other cheeses during their initial period of development, was most often consumed in the country or area where it was developed. Thus, cream cheese is referred to as a fresh, country cheese. However, the cream cheese that appears on the market today is mass-produced in large factories many miles from the source of the milk supply.

Cream cheese was first produced in the United States during the 1870s by a dairyman in New York. About ten years later, commercial production of cream cheese began. Today, it is one of the most popular packaged cheeses in the world.

Soft cream cheese—available in bars and dips.

How cream cheese is produced: A standard procedure for making cream cheese has been developed through mass production. The cream is pasteurized in large vats and quickly cooled. Then a starter of lactic acid bacteria is added to develop the desired acidity and obtain a uniform coagulation. Sometimes rennet is used along with the starter. When coagulation occurs, the curd is heated to express the whey and then mechanical separators separate the whey from the cheese.

After the whey is removed, the cheese is salted and packaged in foil or sealed in jars. This finished cheese-form must contain less than 55% moisture and a minimum of 33% milk fat in order to comply with government standards.

Another soft, unripened cheese, Neufchâtel, is similar to cream cheese both in production and in final form. However, Neufchâtel is higher in moisture and lower in milk fat than cream cheese.

Nutritional value: Two tablespoons of cream cheese supplies 105 calories. Since it is made from cream, it provides many of the milk nutrients such as protein, calcium, phosphorus, the B vitamin riboflavin, and vitamin A. However, cream cheese is most often eaten in small quantities; thus, only small amounts of the above mentioned nutrients are present.

How to select: Cream cheese is available at the dairy counter in the supermarket. Unless sealed in jars, it is most often sold in foil-wrapped packages to prevent loss of moisture. The cheese should be white with no yellowing or evidence of leakage. Sometimes cream cheese is whipped, giving it a lighter, fluffier quality.

The soft, creamy texture of cream cheese blends easily with other ingredients in the preparation of ready-to-serve dips and spreads. Having a mild flavor, cream cheese is usually combined with bacon, clams, shrimp, pimientos, olives, chives, onion, horseradish, Roquefort, blue cheese, pineapple, dates, or nuts.

How to store: Since cream cheese has a relatively high moisture content, it is quite perishable and must be refrigerated. Wrap tightly in moistureproof wrap and use within a few days. Cream cheese may be frozen but will appear slightly dry in texture after thawing.

How to use: The mild, slightly acidic flavor of cream cheese lends itself to a wide variety of uses. Unlike most cheeses, its flavor is more distinct when chilled.

Delicious served alone or with fresh fruit, cream cheese is excellent for use in dips, frostings, spreads, salads, salad dressings, and sauces. Also important in baked products, it is used in cakes, cookies, breads, pies, and refrigerated desserts. Cream cheese is the basic ingredient for the popular cheesecake dessert. When blended with other ingredients, as in making dips or frostings, cream cheese is more easily combined if allowed to soften first at room temperature. (See also *Cheese*.)

Assorted fruits ring-around fluffy Cherry Cream Dressing. Swirl red food coloring in dressing for marbled effect. Accompany with a variety of hot quick breads for a light luncheon.

Cherry-Cream Dressing

1 3-ounce package cream cheese, softened
2 tablespoons mayonnaise or salad dressing
2 tablespoons maraschino cherry juice
1 tablespoon milk
2 teaspoons lemon juice
Few drops red food coloring

• • •

1 2-ounce package dessert topping mix
1 tablespoon finely chopped maraschino cherries

In small mixing bowl combine softened cream cheese, mayonnaise or salad dressing, maraschino cherry juice, milk, lemon juice, and few drops red food coloring. Beat till smooth.

Prepare dessert topping mix according to package directions; fold into cheese mixture. Stir in chopped maraschino cherries. Chill.

To serve, whip chilled dressing till fluffy; pile into serving bowl. Drop one drop red food coloring atop; swirl. Makes about 1⅓ cups.

Cream Cheese Frosting

1 3-ounce package cream cheese, softened
1 tablespoon butter or margarine, softened
1 teaspoon vanilla
2 cups sifted confectioners' sugar
Milk
½ cup chopped pecans (optional)

In small mixing bowl combine softened cream cheese, butter or margarine, and vanilla. Beat at low speed on electric mixer till light. Gradually add sifted confectioners' sugar, beating till fluffy. If necessary, add milk to make frosting of spreading consistency.

Stir in chopped pecans, if desired. Frosts one 8- or 9-inch square cake.

Chocolate-Cream Cheese Frosting: Prepare Cream Cheese Frosting, *except omit vanilla.* Melt one 1-ounce square unsweetened chocolate; cool. Add to cheese with butter. Continue according to recipe directions above.

Shrimp-Cheese Turnovers

½ cup butter or margarine
1 3-ounce package cream cheese, softened
1 cup sifted all-purpose flour
1 5-ounce jar process cheese spread with pimiento
1 4½-ounce can shrimp, drained and cut up

Cut butter and cream cheese into flour till mixture resembles coarse crumbs. Shape dough into a ball; chill 1 hour.

On lightly floured surface roll dough to ⅛ inch thickness; cut in circles with 2-inch round cutter. Dot rounds with cheese spread and sprinkle with cut-up shrimp pieces. Fold over each round into half circle; seal edges.

Bake on *ungreased* baking sheet at 375° till golden brown, about 15 minutes. Makes 36.

Marble Cheesecake

2½ cups crushed vanilla wafers
½ cup butter or margarine, melted
½ cup sugar
1 envelope (1 tablespoon) unflavored gelatin
1 cup milk
1 8-ounce package cream cheese, softened
½ cup sugar
1½ teaspoons vanilla
1 14-ounce can evaporated milk, *chilled icy cold* (1⅔ cups)
¼ cup unsweetened cocoa powder

Combine vanilla wafer crumbs and melted butter. Press on bottom and sides of 9-inch springform pan or 13x9x2-inch baking pan. Chill.

Combine ½ cup sugar and gelatin in saucepan. Stir in 1 cup milk. Heat and stir till sugar and gelatin dissolve. Cool till mixture begins to thicken. Meanwhile, beat together softened cream cheese, ½ cup sugar, and vanilla; blend in thickened gelatin mixture.

Whip *chilled* evaporated milk to stiff peaks; fold into cheese mixture. Place ⅓ of the mixture in small bowl. Gently fold in cocoa. Alternately spoon vanilla and chocolate mixtures into chilled crust; swirl. Chill 8 hours or overnight. Makes 8 to 10 servings.

Cherry-Cheese Dessert Pizza

Plain Pastry for 2-crust 9-inch pie (See *Pastry*)

. . .

1 8-ounce package cream cheese, softened
½ cup sugar
2 eggs
⅓ cup chopped walnuts
1 teaspoon vanilla

. . .

2 21-ounce cans cherry pie filling
Whipped cream cheese *or* whipped cream

On lightly floured surface roll pastry to 14-inch circle; place in 12-inch pizza pan. Flute edges; prick crust. Bake at 350° for 15 minutes. Meanwhile, blend softened cream cheese with sugar; add eggs and beat well. Stir in nuts and vanilla. Pour into partially baked crust and bake 10 minutes longer; cool.

Spread cherry pie filling over cooled cheese layer. Chill. Top chilled pie with dollops of whipped cream cheese *or* whipped cream. To serve, cut in wedges. Makes 10 to 12 servings.

Cream Cheese Cookies

1 cup butter or margarine, softened
2 3-ounce packages cream cheese, softened
1 cup sugar
¼ teaspoon salt
1 teaspoon vanilla
1 egg
2 tablespoons milk
2 cups sifted all-purpose flour
½ cup flaked coconut, toasted
Walnut halves (optional)

In mixing bowl cream together softened butter or margarine, softened cream cheese, sugar, salt, and vanilla. Add egg and milk; beat well. Stir in flour and toasted coconut.

Drop cookie dough from teaspoon onto *ungreased* cookie sheet. Top each cookie with walnut half, if desired. Bake at 325° till done, about 20 minutes. Remove cookies to cooling rack. Makes 5 dozen small cookies.

Fruit Cocktail Smoothee

Prepare one 3¾-ounce package strawberry whipped dessert mix following package directions. Drain one 16-ounce can fruit cocktail, reserving ¾ cup syrup. Add reserved syrup to one 8-ounce package cream cheese, softened; beat smooth. Fold in strawberry dessert.

Prepare one 2-ounce package dessert topping mix following package directions; fold into cream cheese mixture. Chill till partially set; fold in fruit. Spoon into sherbet dishes. Chill 5 to 6 hours. Makes 8 to 10 servings.

CREAMED FOOD—Food served in a white sauce made with milk or a combination of milk and cream. Meat, fish, and poultry are often prepared in this manner and served over toast, noodles, or rice. Vegetables may also be served creamed over toast or as a main dish accompaniment.

Creamed Peas and New Potatoes

1½ pounds tiny new potatoes (about 15)
1 to 1½ cups fresh peas (1 to 1½ pounds in shell)
3 tablespoons sliced green onion
4 tablespoons butter or margarine
4 teaspoons all-purpose flour
1 cup milk

Scrub potatoes; peel off narrow strip around center of each. Cook in boiling, salted water till tender, about 15 to 20 minutes; drain.

Meanwhile, cook peas and onion in small amount of boiling, salted water till tender, about 8 to 15 minutes; drain.

In saucepan melt butter; blend in flour and dash salt. Add milk all at once. Cook quickly, stirring constantly, till mixture thickens and bubbles. Add drained vegetables; heat through. Makes 4 to 6 servings.

A show-off dessert

Convenient canned pie filling tops rich, → creamy cheese layer baked in pastry crust for colorful Cherry-Cheese Dessert Pizza.

These peppermint-flavored, creamy Mint Wafers are made in a jiffy from a frosting mix. Also try different colors and flavors.

CREAM MINT—Small, delicately flavored fondant patties, often softly colored as a key to flavor. Peppermint, lemon, wintergreen, lime, orange, and cinnamon are common flavorings used for these candies. (See also *Fondant.*)

Mint Wafers

3 tablespoons butter or margarine
3 tablespoons milk
1 package creamy white frosting mix (for 2-layer cake)
Several drops oil of peppermint

Melt butter with milk in top of double boiler. Add frosting mix; stir till smooth. Cook over rapidly boiling water for 5 minutes, stirring occasionally. Add flavoring and desired food coloring. Drop from teaspoon onto waxed paper, swirling tops of candies with teaspoon. (Keep candy over hot water while dropping wafers. If mixture thickens, add a few drops hot water.) Cool till firm. Makes 5 dozen.

CREAM OF TARTAR—A powdery white, natural fruit acid (potassium acid tartrate) derived from grapes.

Prior to the introduction of baking powder, cream of tartar was one of the acid ingredients frequently used in combination with baking soda as a leavening agent. Later cream of tartar and baking soda were combined in specific proportions to form baking powder. Cream of tartar is still used as one of the acid ingredients in tartrate baking powder.

The main home uses for cream of tartar are in angel cakes, in candies, and in beating egg whites. Angel cakes containing cream of tartar are whiter and have a finer grain than cakes made without this ingredient. Fondant-type candies are whiter when cream of tartar is added. The addition of small amount of cream of tartar when beating egg whites gives a firmer egg white foam that's more heat stable.

CREAM PIE—A single-crust, cream-filled pie, often topped with a meringue.

The cream filling is thickened with both eggs and starch—cornstarch or flour. Usually, the egg yolks are used in the filling and the egg whites are reserved for the meringue. Milk, water, and fresh or canned fruit juice are the liquid ingredients commonly used in cream fillings.

Since the starch takes longer to thicken than the egg, the starch-liquid part of the filling is cooked briefly before the egg is added. The filling is then cooked a few minutes more to cook the egg.

> ***Cooking cream pie fillings***
>
> Cook cream fillings only the specified time. Overcooking causes the starch to break down and lose its thickening power.

Although the basic cream filling is usually vanilla, banana, coconut, or almond flavorings may be added for variety. Other popular variations include butterscotch, chocolate, and lemon cream pies. A fluffy meringue or a thick layer of whipped cream adds the final touch to a cream pie.

Cream pies that are allowed to stand without refrigeration are quite susceptible to food poisoning organisms. Therefore, it is particularly important to store cream pies in the refrigerator promptly. Most cream pies, however, cannot be frozen satisfactorily. (See also *Pie*.)

Banana-Apricot Pie

2 cups snipped dried apricots
1¼ cups sugar
3 tablespoons all-purpose flour
3 beaten egg yolks
2 tablespoons butter or margarine
2 medium bananas, sliced (2 cups)
1 *baked* 9-inch pastry shell, cooled
Meringue

Combine apricots and 1½ cups water. Cover; simmer till tender, about 10 minutes. Combine sugar, flour, and ¼ teaspoon salt; stir into apricot mixture. Cook till boiling; boil 2 minutes, stirring constantly. Stir small amount hot mixture into egg yolks; return to hot mixture. Cook and stir till boiling. Stir in butter.

Place sliced bananas in bottom of pastry shell; top with apricot filling. Spread Meringue over hot filling; seal to edge. Bake at 350° for 12 to 15 minutes. Cool before serving.

Meringue: Beat 3 egg whites with ½ teaspoon vanilla and ¼ teaspoon cream of tartar till soft peaks form. Gradually add 6 tablespoons sugar, beating till stiff and glossy peaks form and all of the sugar is dissolved.

Strawberry-Pineapple Cream Pie

1 3- *or* 3¼-ounce package *regular* vanilla pudding mix
1½ cups milk
1 8¾-ounce can crushed pineapple, well drained (⅔ cup)
1 teaspoon vanilla
½ cup whipping cream
1 *baked* 9-inch pastry shell, cooled

• • •

3 cups fresh strawberries
½ cup water
¼ cup sugar
2 teaspoons cornstarch
Red food coloring

Prepare vanilla pudding mix according to package directions *using the 1½ cups milk*. Cool slightly without stirring. Fold in drained pineapple and vanilla. Whip cream; fold into vanilla pudding mixture. Spread in cooled, baked pastry shell. Chill till set.

In small saucepan crush *½ cup* of the fresh strawberries; add water. Cook 2 minutes and sieve. Combine sugar and cornstarch; gradually stir in sieved berries. Return mixture to saucepan and cook, stirring constantly, till mixture is thickened and clear. Tint to desired color with red food coloring.

Slice remaining fresh strawberries in half lengthwise, reserving a few perfect whole strawberries for center of pie. Arrange sliced berries over cream filling; spoon strawberry glaze over. Chill several hours. Serve topped with dollop of whipped cream, if desired.

Stir small amount of hot mixture into beaten egg yolks. Slowly add to hot mixture.

Pour hot cream filling into cooled, baked pastry shell; top with fluffy meringue.

To prevent meringue from shrinking, carefully seal to edge of pastry all around.

Lemonade Meringue Pie

A refreshingly different pie—

1 cup dairy sour cream
3 slightly beaten egg yolks
1 4½- or 5-ounce package regular vanilla pudding mix
1¼ cups milk
⅓ cup frozen lemonade concentrate, thawed

• • •

1 9-inch *baked* pastry shell, cooled
Meringue

In saucepan combine diary sour cream and egg yolks. Stir in vanilla pudding mix, milk, and lemonade concentrate. Cook, stirring constantly, till mixture thickens and boils. Remove from heat; spoon into cooled pastry shell. Spread Meringue atop hot filling, sealing to edges of pastry. Bake at 350° till golden brown, about 12 to 15 minutes. Cool; chill.

Meringue: Beat 3 egg whites, ½ teaspoon vanilla, and ¼ teaspoon cream of tartar till soft peaks form. Gradually add 6 tablespoons sugar, beating to stiff peaks. Spread on pie.

Chocolate Truffle Pie

2 cups milk
2 1-ounce squares unsweetened chocolate, broken
1 cup sugar
¼ cup cornstarch
¼ teaspoon salt
2 eggs
1½ teaspoons vanilla

• • •

1 9-inch unbaked pastry shell
Whipped cream

In saucepan heat milk and chocolate over medium-low heat, stirring till blended. In bowl combine sugar, cornstarch, and salt. Beat eggs just till blended; add to sugar mixture along with vanilla. Stir to blend. Gradually stir in chocolate mixture. Pour into pastry shell.

Bake at 400° for 35 minutes, covering crust with foil during last 10 to 15 minutes. Cool. (Filling will thicken somewhat on cooling.) Garnish with dollops of whipped cream.

Orange Meringue Pie

¾ cup sugar
¼ cup cornstarch
1½ cups orange juice
2 slightly beaten egg yolks
1 tablespoon butter or margarine
1 teaspoon grated orange peel
1 8-inch *baked* pastry shell, cooled

• • •

2 egg whites
¼ cup sugar

In saucepan combine the ¾ cup sugar, the cornstarch, and ¼ teaspoon salt. Gradually stir in orange juice. Cook and stir over high heat till thickened and bubbly. Reduce heat. Cook 1 minute more; remove from heat. Stir small amount hot mixture into egg yolks; return to hot mixture. Cook and stir over medium heat 2 minutes more. Stir in butter and orange peel. Pour into pastry shell.

Beat egg whites to soft peaks; gradually beat in the ¼ cup sugar till stiff peaks form. Spread meringue over hot filling, sealing to edge of crust. Bake at 400° till golden brown, about 7 to 9 minutes. Let cool on rack before serving.

Spiced Butterscotch Pie

1 stick piecrust mix
¼ cup finely chopped nuts
1 4-ounce package regular butterscotch pudding mix
½ teaspoon ground cinnamon
¼ teaspoon ground nutmeg
Dash ground ginger
½ cup whipping cream

Prepare pastry according to package directions. Roll out and sprinkle with nuts; roll lightly to press in. Fit pastry into 8-inch pie plate; flute edge. With a fork, prick bottom and sides. Bake according to package directions; cool.

In saucepan combine butterscotch pudding mix, ground cinnamon, ground nutmeg, and ground ginger. Cook according to package directions. Cool 5 minutes; turn into pastry shell. Cover surface of pudding with waxed paper. Chill. Remove waxed paper from pie. Whip cream; spread atop pie. Sprinkle with additional chopped nuts, if desired.

Mince Cream Pie

1½ cups prepared mincemeat
1 8-inch *baked* pastry shell, cooled

. . .

1 3x1½-inch strip orange peel
1½ cups milk
1 3¾- or 3⅝-ounce package *instant* vanilla pudding mix
Ground nutmeg

Spoon prepared mincemeat into cooled pastry shell. Place orange peel in blender container; cover and turn blender on and off quickly to chop peel. Add milk and *instant* vanilla pudding mix to chopped orange peel in blender container. Cover; blend 5 seconds.

Pour pudding mixture over mincemeat in pastry shell; sprinkle with a little ground nutmeg. Chill thoroughly before serving.

Cherry Cream Pie

In saucepan combine ¾ cup sugar, 3 tablespoons cornstarch, and ¼ teaspoon salt. Gradually stir in 2 cups milk. Cook over medium-high heat, stirring till mixture thickens and bubbles. Cook and stir 1 minute longer. Remove from heat. Stir small amount of hot mixture into 2 slightly beaten eggs. Return to hot mixture; cook 2 minutes longer, stirring constantly. Remove from heat. Stir in 2 tablespoons butter or margarine and 1 teaspoon vanilla. Pour the mixture into one 9-inch *baked* pastry shell. Chill thoroughly.

Stir ¼ teaspoon almond extract into one 21-ounce can cherry pie filling. Spoon over cream filling. Chill pie thoroughly.

CREAM PUFF—Light, hollow puff filled with a sweet, savory filling. In France, cream puff pastry is called *chou* which literally means "cabbage." This name is applied because the finished puff vaguely resembles a miniature cabbage.

Although classed as a pastry, cream puffs are quite different from other types of pastry. They contain a large proportion of fat and eggs and are leavened by steam. The fat is responsible for the tenderness of cream puffs, and the eggs help to form the shell of the puff structure.

The most frequent criticism of cream puffs concerns sunken puffs. When the baked puffs are removed from the oven, they are golden brown and puffy. Their structure, however, is still very delicate and may collapse. This can be prevented by immediately puncturing or splitting each puff and returning it to the still-warm oven to dry out. Even after drying, the puff may have a slightly soggy center. This excess membrane may be removed, if desired, to leave a crisp, hollow puff.

Because their puffs always fall, many homemakers consider cream puffs difficult to make, and avoid doing so. However, once the technique for making them has been mastered, cream puffs become a versatile food that can be used as the basis for appetizers, main dishes, or desserts.

Cream Puffs

½ cup butter or margarine
1 cup sifted all-purpose flour
¼ teaspoon salt
4 eggs

In saucepan melt butter or margarine in 1 cup boiling water. Add flour and salt all at once; stir vigorously. Cook and stir till mixture forms a ball that doesn't separate. Remove from heat; cool slightly. Add eggs, one at a time, beating after each till smooth.

Drop by heaping tablespoons, 3 inches apart, on greased baking sheet. Bake at 450° for 15 minutes, then at 325° for 25 minutes. Remove from oven; split. Turn oven off; put cream puffs back in to dry, about 20 minutes. Cool on rack. Makes 10 cream puffs.

These delight-filled puffs can be tightly covered and stored for a short time in the refrigerator. Unfilled cream puffs can be frozen for longer periods of storage.

By varying the size and filling, cream puffs can be a dainty appetizer, a hearty main dish, or a luscious dessert. Miniature puffs filled with cheese spread, seafood salad, or other savory ingredients start any meal out right. Man-sized puffs overflowing with an à la king or meat salad will satisfy even the heartiest appetite.

For an elegant dessert, serve Custard-Filled Cream Puffs topped with rich Chocolate Sauce and chopped nuts. Use the extra Chocolate Sauce to make ice cream sundaes.

Cream puffs are most often used as a dessert. A crisp puff filled with a cream filling and topped with a smooth sauce is a big favorite with many people. For a lighter dessert, fill puffs with whipped cream. Cream puffs add a special touch to any meal. (See also *Dessert*.)

Ham and Eggs in Caraway Puffs

¼ cup butter or margarine
½ cup sifted all-purpose flour
2 eggs
2 teaspoons caraway seed
3 tablespoons butter or margarine
3 tablespoons all-purpose flour
2 cups milk
1 cup cubed fully cooked ham
4 hard-cooked eggs, sliced
1 tablespoon chopped canned pimiento
¼ cup chopped green pepper

In small saucepan melt the ¼ cup butter or margarine in ½ cup boiling water. Add the ½ cup all-purpose flour and ⅛ teaspoon salt; stir vigorously. Cook and stir till mixture forms a ball that doesn't separate. Remove from heat and cool slightly. Add 2 eggs, one at a time, beating vigorously after each till mixture is smooth. Stir in caraway seed.

Drop dough by heaping tablespoons, 3 inches apart, on greased baking sheet. Bake at 450° for 15 minutes, then at 325° for 25 minutes. Remove cream puffs from the oven; split. Turn oven off and put cream puffs back in oven to dry, about 20 minutes.

Meanwhile, for filling, melt 3 tablespoons butter or margarine in saucepan over low heat. Blend in 3 tablespoons flour, ½ teaspoon salt, and dash pepper. Add milk all at once. Cook quickly, stirring constantly, till mixture thickens and bubbles. Add cubed ham, sliced hard-cooked eggs, chopped pimiento, and chopped green pepper; heat through. Spoon into cream puffs; serve immediately. Serves 4 or 5.

Custard-Filled Cream Puffs

Cream Puffs (see page 691 for recipe)
⅔ cup sugar
2 tablespoons all-purpose flour
2 tablespoons cornstarch
½ teaspoon salt
3 cups milk
2 slightly beaten egg yolks
2 teaspoons vanilla
1 cup whipping cream
Chocolate Sauce

Prepare cream puffs; bake. Split and return to oven to dry; cool.

In saucepan combine sugar, flour, cornstarch, and salt. Gradually stir in milk. Cook and stir till mixture thickens and boils; cook and stir 2 to 3 minutes longer. Stir a little hot mixture into slightly beaten egg yolks; return to hot mixture. Cook and stir till mixture just boils. Add vanilla; cool. Beat smooth. Whip cream; fold into cooled mixture.

Fill cream puffs with cooled filling. Top with Chocolate Sauce. Makes 10 puffs.

Chocolate Sauce: In small saucepan melt three 1-ounce squares unsweetened chocolate; cool. In saucepan combine 1 cup sugar, ¾ cup water, and ½ cup light corn syrup; bring to boiling. Gradually add hot mixture to melted chocolate, blending well. Boil gently 10 to 15 minutes, stirring occasionally. Add 1 teaspoon vanilla. Cover entire surface with clear plastic wrap; cool. Makes 1⅔ cups sauce.

Chocolate-Pecan Cream Puffs

½ cup butter or margarine
1 cup sifted all-purpose flour
3 tablespoons unsweetened cocoa powder
1 tablespoon sugar
4 eggs
½ cup chopped pecans
Coffee ice cream
Marshmallow Sauce

Melt butter or margarine in 1 cup boiling water. Sift together flour, ¼ teaspoon salt, cocoa powder, and sugar. Add to butter-water mixture all at once; stir vigorously. Cook, stirring constantly, till mixture forms a ball that does not separate. Remove from heat; cool slightly. Add eggs, one at a time, beating vigorously after each till smooth. Stir in pecans.

Drop dough by heaping tablespoons onto greased baking sheet. Bake at 450° for 10 minutes, then at 325° for 20 minutes. Remove from oven; split. Turn oven off; return puffs to oven to dry, about 20 minutes. Remove excess soft centers. Cool. At serving time, fill with ice cream; top with Marshmallow Sauce. Makes 10.

Marshmallow Sauce: In 2-quart saucepan combine 1½ cups sugar, 1 cup light cream, ¼ pound marshmallows (16 to 20), and dash salt. Cook and stir till mixture is boiling; then cook over medium heat till candy thermometer reaches 224°, about 8 to 10 minutes. Remove from heat; add ¼ cup butter or margarine. Cool slightly; stir in 1 teaspoon vanilla.

Follow these steps for perfect cream puffs. Add the butter to boiling water. Add flour and salt at the same time.

Cook, stirring vigorously, till mixture forms a smooth ball. Remove from heat; vigorously beat in eggs, one at a time.

Drop dough by spoonfuls onto greased baking sheet. Bake. Split puffs. Turn off oven; return to oven to dry. Cool.

CREAM SAUCE—A thick sauce made with cream or milk, flour, butter or margarine, and seasonings. It has the consistency of a standard, medium white sauce. Cream sauce is served over vegetables, eggs, fish, and poultry. (See also *Sauce.*)

CREAM SODA—A soft drink made with carbonated water. Vanilla and caramel give flavor and a brown color to the drink.

CREAM SOUP—A soup similar to thin white sauce with vegetable juice, vegetable pulp, or broth from meat, fish, or poultry substituted for part or all of the milk.

Cream soups are thickened with cornstarch, rice, or vegetables. The vegetables are cooked until tender, puréed, and blended with the other ingredients. Or, grated, raw vegetables are added to a white sauce and the mixture is heated to boiling. Seasonings are added, such as onion, parsley, herbs, and spices. Garnishes of parsley, grated cheese, toasted bread crumbs, and pimiento are sprinkled on top.

Serve cream soups either hot or cold as an appetizer or as part of the main course with sandwiches. (See also *Soup.*)

Cream of Tomato Soup

Great with grilled sandwiches—

1 28-ounce can tomatoes
2 slices onion
1 bay leaf
1 teaspoon sugar
1 teaspoon salt
1/4 teaspoon pepper

• • •

2 tablespoons butter or margarine
2 tablespoons all-purpose flour
1 1/2 cups milk

Combine tomatoes, onion, bay leaf, sugar, salt, and pepper in a 2-quart saucepan. Simmer 10 minutes; sieve. Prepare white sauce by melting butter in saucepan over low heat. Blend in flour and add milk all at once. Cook quickly, stirring constantly, till mixture is thickened and bubbly. Remove sauce from heat and slowly add hot tomato mixture, stirring constantly. Serve at once. Makes 6 servings.

Chilled Cream of Chive Soup

3 tablespoons butter or margarine
3 tablespoons all-purpose flour
1 14-ounce can chicken broth (1 3/4 cups)
1 bay leaf
2 tablespoons finely snipped chives
1 cup light cream

In saucepan melt butter; blend in flour. Add broth all at once. Add bay leaf and chives. Cook and stir over medium heat till thickened and bubbly. Remove bay leaf. Stir in cream; chill thoroughly. Serve cold. Serves 6.

Cream of Potato Soup

2 tablespoons butter or margarine
2 tablespoons all-purpose flour
1/2 teaspoon salt
Dash white pepper
3 cups milk
2 cups diced, cooked potatoes
1 tablespoon chopped canned pimiento

Melt butter in saucepan over low heat. Blend in flour, salt, and white pepper. Add milk all at once. Cook quickly, stirring constantly, till mixture is thickened and bubbly. Add potatoes and pimiento; heat through. Season to taste with salt and white pepper. Makes 6 servings.

Chicken Velvet Soup

6 tablespoons butter or margarine
1/3 cup all-purpose flour
1/2 cup milk
1/2 cup light cream
3 cups chicken broth
1 cup finely chopped cooked chicken

Melt butter or margarine in saucepan. Blend in flour; add milk, cream, and broth. Cook and stir till mixture thickens and comes to a boil; reduce heat. Stir in chicken and dash pepper. Heat again just to boiling; serve immediately. Garnish with snipped parsley and pimiento, if desired. Serves 4.

Start the meal with an appetizer of cold soup. Place Chilled Cream of Chive Soup in bowls surrounded by cracked ice for an attractive serving idea and to keep the right temperature.

CREAMY—A term indicating a soft, smooth texture. A creamy food resembles cream in appearance, consistency, or flavor.

CREME ***(krem, krēm, krām)***—1. Cream or cream sauce. 2. A French term for whipped cream or butter and custard used in desserts, such as Crème Brûlét. 3. A liqueur.

There are numerous flavors of crème liqueur. Some of the better-known flavors are *crème de menthe* flavored with mint, *crème de cacao* with cocoa and vanilla, *crème de cassis* with black currants, *crème de fraise* with strawberries, and *crème de café* with coffee. These liqueurs are clear and are available colored or colorless.

Crèmes are used as a drink, especially for an after-dinner drink. The liqueur can be served "straight," over cracked ice as a frappé, or in mixed cocktails. Grasshoppers and stingers are examples of cocktails made with *crème de menthe*. Brandy Alexander and angel's dream are made with *crème de cacao* as an ingredient.

Other uses for crèmes are as a dessert topping and as an ingredient in a dessert. Pour a crème over ice cream, sherbet, fruit, or pastry. Choose a flavor that complements the basic dessert. Good examples of this are *crème de menthe* over lemon sherbet or over a chocolate brownie and *crème d' ananas*, a pineapple-flavored crème, over chunks of mixed, chilled fruit.

As an ingredient, the cremes flavor pies, cookies, candies, and desserts. Examples of specialties made with cremes are grasshopper pie and bananas foster. The first combines the flavor of the grasshopper drink with the fluffy texture of chiffon pie. The bananas foster, a delightful specialty made with *creme de bananes*, is flambeed. (See also *Liqueur*.)

Crème de Menthe Balls

2½ cups finely crushed vanilla wafers (about 60)
1 cup sifted confectioners' sugar
2 tablespoons unsweetened cocoa powder
1 cup finely chopped walnuts
¼ cup light corn syrup
¼ cup white crème de menthe
Granulated sugar

Combine wafer crumbs, confectioners' sugar, cocoa, and walnuts. Stir in corn syrup and crème de menthe. Add a few drops of water, if necessary, to form mixture into 1-inch balls. Roll in granulated sugar. Store in tightly covered container. Makes 42 balls.

Chocolate-Mint Dessert

½ cup graham cracker crumbs
2 tablespoons butter or margarine, melted

• • •

½ cup sugar
1 envelope unflavored gelatin
2 tablespoons cornstarch
2 cups milk
3 slightly beaten egg yolks

• • •

3 egg whites
¼ cup sugar
½ cup whipping cream
1½ teaspoons crème de menthe
2 1-ounce squares unsweetened chocolate, melted

Blend cracker crumbs and melted butter. Reserve 1 tablespoon; spread remainder in 10x6x1½-inch baking dish. Combine the ½ cup sugar, gelatin, and cornstarch; add milk. Cook and stir till boiling. Add small amount of hot mixture to egg yolks; return to hot mixture. Cook 1 minute. Cool till partially thickened.

Beat egg whites to soft peaks; gradually add the ¼ cup sugar. Beat to stiff peaks. Fold into custard. Whip cream; fold into custard. Remove 1½ cups mixture; add crème de menthe. Stir chocolate into remaining mixture. Spread half the chocolate mixture over crumbs; cover with mint layer, then remaining chocolate. Top with reserved crumbs. Chill till firm. Serves 6.

Lazy Grasshopper Pie

Make one 3¾-ounce package vanilla whipped dessert mix according to package directions. Stir in 2 tablespoons green crème de menthe and 1 tablespoon white crème de cacao. Chill till mixture mounds slightly. Pile into *baked* 8-inch pastry shell. Chill. Trim with whipped dessert topping and chocolate curls.

CRÈME BRÛLÉE ***(krem brü lā')***—A dessert of baked custard topped with caramelized sugar or a caramel sauce. Crème brûlée is a contrast of flavors and textures—rich, creamy custard covered with the brittle, slightly bitter crust of burnt sugar.

Crème Brûlée

2 slightly beaten eggs
2 slightly beaten egg yolks
¼ cup sugar
¼ teaspoon salt
2 cups light cream, scalded
½ teaspoon vanilla
2 egg whites
Dash salt
¼ cup sugar
1 cup sugar

Crenshaw melons, weighing from four to nine pounds, have spicy, pink orange meat surrounded by a thin, green and yellow rind.

In top of double boiler, combine whole eggs, egg yolks, ¼ cup sugar, and ¼ teaspoon salt. Slowly stir in cream. Cook, stirring constantly, over *gently boiling* water, till custard coats metal spoon; cook 2 minutes more. Cool at once, placing pan in sink or a bowl of cold water and stirring for a minute or two. Stir in vanilla. Pour custard mixture into shallow 1½-quart dish; chill.

Combine egg whites and salt; beat to soft peaks. Gradually add ¼ cup sugar, beating to stiff peaks. In skillet heat 3 cups water to a gentle simmer. *Do not boil.* Drop meringue in 6 puffs onto water. Cook, uncovered, till set, about 5 minutes; drain on paper toweling. Arrange poached meringues on custard.

In heavy skillet cook and stir the 1 cup sugar over low heat till sugar melts and forms a syrup. Immediately drizzle from tip of spoon over custard and meringue puffs. Serves 6.

CRÈME PATISSERIE ***(puh ti' suhr ē)***—A cream or custard filling used with pastries such as cream puffs.

CRENSHAW—A globe-shaped melon which is a hybrid variety of muskmelon. The crenshaw has a rounded base and a pointed, slightly wrinkled stem end. The smooth rind with no netting and little ribbing has a green color when immature but turns yellow as it ripens. The thick, juicy flesh of the crenshaw has a full, slightly spicy aroma and rich flavor.

Crenshaw melons are available on the market from July to October. Select ripe melons, those with a yellow gold rind, distinct aroma, and softening at the blossom end. Because these melons are very perishable, cover in clear plastic wrap or plastic bags and refrigerate as soon as purchased. Use within two or three days.

Serve slices and halves of crenshaw as desserts or salads, alone or mixed with other fruits. (See also *Melon*.)

Fancy custard for dessert

Drizzling caramelized sugar over the velvety custard and snowy puffs of meringue, puts the finishing touches to Crème Brûlée.

CREOLE COOKERY ***(krē' ōl)***—A cuisine developed in Louisiana and the Gulf States by the Creoles. The food has a unique style influenced by the people, the climate, and the geography of this area.

Creoles are the descendants of the French and Spanish settlers in America. "Creative person" is the Latin translation of Creole, and these persons were indeed creative. They took the best of the French cuisine, borrowed the spicy Spanish seasonings, and incorporated the foods familiar to the American Indians in the Gulf area. All of these were then modified by the remarkably patient Negro cooks who brought their basic cooking techniques with them from Africa.

The foods of Creole cookery are highly seasoned as are the foods in most tropical climates. Creole dishes are often very spicy and very hot, yet the seasonings are balanced so that no one flavor asserts itself over any other flavor.

Because Creole cookery developed along the Mississippi River and the Gulf Coast, fish and shellfish predominate in Creole dishes. The people also took advantage of other native foods in their area. Game and vegetables, such as okra and yams, were used extensively. Rice became the basic starch food and tomatoes a common ingredient in sauces. One of the local seasonings, filé, was introduced to the settlers by the Choctaw Indians. Filé is made of powdered young sassafras leaves and is used in seafood dishes and gumbos to impart the texture of okra.

The Creoles, thus, developed an authentic American cuisine, a blend of the best from the Old and New Worlds.

Typical Creole dishes: The main dishes in Creole cuisine have a number of common ingredients. Most are a combination of rice, tomatoes, onions, and garlic with the seafoods, poultry, and game of the Gulf area. Bay leaves, thyme, hot pepper sauce (a mixture of vinegar and red peppers developed in Louisiana), and filé produce the highly seasoned flavors.

The basis for most Creole cookery is the *roux*. This is a cooked mixture of flour and shortening, sometimes cooked until brown. Then liquids are added. This sauce, unlike gravy and white sauce, is made at the beginning rather that at the end of the preparation of a dish.

A dish such as Shrimp Creole illustrates the Creole-style of cooking. It is a highly seasoned combination of tomato sauce, onion, green peppers (sometimes called bell peppers by the Creoles), and the popular seafood in a dish to be served with rice.

Shrimp Creole

½ cup chopped onion
½ cup chopped celery
1 clove garlic, minced
3 tablespoons shortening

• • •

1 16-ounce can tomatoes
1 8-ounce can tomato sauce
1½ teaspoons salt
1 teaspoon sugar
1 tablespoon Worcestershire sauce
½ to 1 teaspoon chili powder
Dash bottled hot pepper sauce

• • •

2 teaspoons cornstarch
1 tablespoon cold water
12 ounces frozen shelled shrimp, thawed
½ cup chopped green pepper
Parsley Rice Ring

In skillet cook onion, celery, and garlic in shortening till tender but not brown. Add tomatoes, tomato sauce, salt, sugar, Worcestershire sauce, chili powder, and pepper sauce. Simmer, uncovered, 45 minutes. Mix cornstarch with cold water; stir into sauce. Cook and stir till mixture is thickened and bubbly. Add shrimp and green pepper. Cover; simmer 5 minutes. Serve with Parsley Rice Ring. Serves 6.

Parsley Rice Ring: Combine 3 cups hot cooked rice with ¼ cup snipped parsley. Pack into an *ungreased* 5½-cup ring mold. Turn out at once on warm platter.

Creole elegance

Simmer tomato sauce in piquant seasonings → as a rich background for shrimp. Serving Shrimp Creole over rice ring makes the meal.

Specific examples of Creole dishes are the famous jambalayas and gumbos. Jambalaya is a rice dish cooked with tomatoes, onions, herbs, and seafood, meat, or poultry. This dish was probably introduced when the Spanish controlled New Orleans since it resembles the Spanish dish, *paella*. It is eaten as a casserole or a stew.

Jambalaya, a tossed salad, and corn bread or French bread make a complete menu for a lunch or a light supper.

Crab Jambalaya

6 slices bacon
½ cup chopped onion
½ cup chopped celery
¼ cup chopped green pepper

• • •

1 28-ounce can tomatoes
¼ cup uncooked long-grain rice
1 teaspoon Worcestershire sauce
½ teaspoon salt
Dash pepper
1 7½-ounce can crab meat, drained, flaked, and cartilage removed

Cook bacon till crisp; drain, reserving 2 tablespoons drippings. Crumble bacon; set aside. Cook onion, celery, and green pepper in reserved drippings till tender. Cut up tomatoes. Add tomatoes and juice, rice, Worcestershire sauce, salt, and pepper to vegetables. Simmer, covered, till rice is tender, about 20 to 25 minutes, stirring occasionally. Add crab; heat through. Spoon into serving bowl; top with reserved bacon. Makes 4 to 6 servings.

Gumbo resembles a thick soup made with a wide assortment of meat or shellfish, tomatoes, and okra. The name comes from this last ingredient because gumbo is derived from the African word for okra.

Filé is commonly used in gumbo as a substitute for the slippery, smooth texture of okra. Care must be taken that the filé is never cooked because it will become stringy. The spice should be stirred in only when cooking is complete.

A variation of the basic type of gumbo is the *gumbo z'herbs*. This dish contains fresh greens and seasonings.

Gumbo Z'Herbs

½ pound salt pork, finely chopped
1 small head cabbage, quartered
1 bunch spinach, torn
½ bunch turnip greens, torn
½ bunch mustard greens, torn

• • •

1 tablespoon shortening
1 small onion, minced
2 cloves garlic, minced
1 tablespoon flour
1 tablespoon vinegar
1 pod red pepper, broken, *or* dash cayenne pepper

Cover pork with water; cover pan and simmer about ½ hour. Drain. Place cabbage, spinach, turnip greens, and mustard greens in large kettle and cover with water; cook till greens are tender, about 7 to 10 minutes. Drain and reserve liquid. Put vegetables in blender container and blend until smooth, or mince finely.

In 3-quart saucepan, melt shortening. Add onion and garlic; cook till tender. Blend in flour. Add greens and salt pork. Stir in enough reserved vegetable liquid to make a thick purée (about 3 cups). Add vinegar, ¾ teaspoon salt, and cayenne. Makes 6 servings.

Gumbo, like jambalaya, is eaten as a main course dish requiring little else to make the meal a complete Creole feast.

Jambalaya and gumbo are frequently made with leftovers or odds and ends of food. This illustrates a trait of the Creoles —they do not waste food, but use leftovers to make many delectable dishes.

Creoles are famous for their many fine soups. Their *bouillabaisse* has been appraised as finer than any soup found in France. Turtle soups, thick and thin seafood mixtures, and bisque of shellfish or game are among a few of their specialties.

Creole Clam Bisque

Combine one 10¾-ounce can condensed clam chowder (Manhattan style), one 10½-ounce can condensed chicken gumbo, and 1 can light cream in a saucepan. Cook till heated through. Makes 4 or 5 servings.

Creole cookery, like French cookery, uses sauces extensively. These sauces usually begin with *roux,* then fish or chicken broth, milk, or wine is added for flavor. Meat, fish, and poultry are frequently cooked in a sauce or served with a sauce, such as the following Creole Sauce:

Creole Sauce

¼ cup finely chopped onion
3 tablespoons finely chopped green pepper
1 tablespoon butter or margarine

. . .

1 8-ounce can tomato sauce
1 3-ounce can chopped mushrooms, drained
¼ cup water
Dash pepper
Dash garlic salt

Cook onion and green pepper in butter till tender. Add tomato sauce, mushrooms, water, pepper, and garlic salt. Cover and simmer 15 minutes. Serve with fish. Makes 1½ cups.

French ancestry is reflected in other Creole foods as well as in the sauces. Many of the desserts are basically French. *Brioche,* a soft roll, and *beignet,* a sweet fritter, are typical French foods incorporated into Creole cuisine.

Other desserts are credited to the Creole's own culture. Calas, for instance, are Creole cakes made with rice and yeast, and fried. Many years ago, these cakes were sold by Negro vendors in the streets of the *Vieux Carré,* the French Quarter of New Orleans. People returning from early Sunday church services would stop to hear the vendors' songs and buy these cakes to take home for their breakfast.

Rich chocolate cake and pralines are also typical Creole desserts. The chocolate cakes are made with brown sugar and sometimes strong coffee to produce an especially tempting flavor. Pralines, made of brown or granulated sugar, cream, and pecans, are a traditional Creole favorite which many tourists choose to send home as souvenirs of their visit to New Orleans.

To temper the sweetness of these desserts, Creole coffee with its strong, rich, chicory flavor can be served. The bite of chicory is often softened by making *café au lait* with hot milk or *café brûlot* with citrus peel, spices, and brandy.

CREPE ***(krāp)***—A thin, delicate pancake. The crepe batter is made of eggs, butter, flour, and milk and may be either sweetened or unsweetened. The sweet ones with fruit or custard fillings and sauces are used for desserts. Unsweetened crepes are filled with meat, vegetables, or cheese and served as appetizers or main dishes. Crepes, cut in strips or V-shapes, make interesting garnishes for soups. This is an excellent way to use leftover crepes.

The technique of making crepes can be mastered with the proper utensils and practice. Crepes are cooked in a small,

Taste the excellence of delicate crepes and almond cream filling together in Crepes Frangipane, a treat for all to remember.

heavy skillet. There are special pans on the market with flaired sides. However, a standard six-inch skillet can be used.

To cook the pancakes, butter and heat the skillet. Remove from heat, pour in about two tablespoons batter, and quickly tilt pan so the batter covers the bottom. Now, return pan to heat and brown crepe on just one side. Remove from pan and repeat. When ready to serve, fill the crepes, but remember to place the filling on the side which was not browned so the attractive side shows. (See also *Pancake*.)

Avoid last-minute steps

Crepes can be made ahead of time and stacked with a sheet of waxed paper between each. Refrigerate or freeze the crepes until they are needed.

Crepes Frangipane

1/3 cup sifted all-purpose flour
1 tablespoon sugar
1 egg
1 egg yolk
3/4 cup milk
1 tablespoon butter, melted
Almond Cream Filling
2 tablespoons butter, melted
1/2 of 1-ounce square unsweetened chocolate, grated
Confectioners' sugar

Combine first 6 ingredients and dash salt in blender container or mixing bowl. Blend or beat with electric or rotary beater till smooth. Lightly grease a 6-inch skillet; heat till drop of water dances on surface. Lift skillet off heat and pour in 2 tablespoons batter. Quickly tilt from side to side till batter covers bottom evenly. Return skillet to heat and cook till underside is lightly browned, about 1 1/2 minutes. To remove, invert skillet over paper toweling. Repeat.

Spread about 3 tablespoons of Almond Cream Filling on unbrowned side of each crepe; roll up and place folded side down in 13x9x2-inch baking dish. Brush crepes with the 2 tablespoons melted butter and bake at 350° till hot, about 20 to 25 minutes. Sprinkle tops of crepes with chocolate and sift confectioners' sugar over all. To serve spoon whipped cream over warm crepes. Makes 10 crepes.

Almond Cream Filling

1 cup sugar
1/4 cup all-purpose flour
1 cup milk
2 eggs
2 egg yolks
3 tablespoons butter or margarine
2 teaspoons vanilla
1/2 teaspoon almond extract
1/2 cup ground toasted almonds

Mix sugar and flour. Add milk; cook and stir till thickened, then continue cooking and stirring 1 or 2 minutes longer. Beat eggs and egg yolks slightly; stir some of hot mixture into eggs and return to hot mixture. Cook and stir just to boiling and remove from heat. Beat smooth. Stir in butter, vanilla, almond extract, and almonds. Cool to room temperature.

Ignite brandy in a long-handled ladle and spoon over Ham-Apricot Crepes just before serving. It's a dramatic show for brunch.

Ham-Apricot Crepes

Make crepes and sauce ahead, then combine with ham at serving time—

1 egg
1 cup milk
1 tablespoon butter or margarine, melted
1 cup sifted all-purpose flour
10 thin slices boiled ham
1 8-ounce can apricot halves
2/3 cup sugar
2 tablespoons cornstarch
Dash salt
1 12-ounce can apricot nectar (1 1/2 cups)
2 teaspoons lemon juice
2 tablespoons butter or margarine

Beat egg just enough to blend. Add milk, the 1 tablespoon melted butter, and flour; beat till smooth. Lightly grease a 6-inch skillet; heat. Remove from heat and pour 2 tablespoons batter into skillet; quickly tilt pan from side to side till batter covers bottom. Return to heat; brown crepe on one side only. Repeat with remaining batter to make 10 crepes.

Drain apricots, reserving syrup. Place a ham slice on unbrowned side of each crepe; roll up with a ham slice inside. Place in chafing dish or skillet with apricot halves. Pour Apricot Sauce over all; cover and heat through. Keep warm till ready to serve.

Apricot Sauce: Mix sugar, cornstarch, and salt. Blend in reserved apricot syrup. Add nectar. Cook and stir till slightly thickened and clear. Remove from heat; add lemon juice. Stir in the 2 tablespoons butter till melted.

CREPES SUZETTE ***(krāp sōō zet')***—An exquisite dessert made of thin pancakes with an orange-flavored sauce or filling. Crepes Suzette is usually flamed with a liqueur or brandy when served.

The crepes can be made ahead; then, just before serving, roll or fold and heat them in the sauce. Or, the orange-flavored sauce can be spread inside the crepes before they are rolled. The heating and flaming of Crepes Suzette is a spectacular scene to enjoy in restaurants or to perform at home for special occasions.

Crepes Suzette

Delicate pancakes with orange filling—

2/3 cup sifted all-purpose flour
2 tablespoons sugar
1/8 teaspoon salt
2 eggs
2 egg yolks
1 1/2 cups milk
2 tablespoons butter or margarine, melted

. . .

1/2 cup butter or margarine
1/2 cup sugar
2 teaspoons grated orange peel
1 teaspoon lemon peel
1/4 cup orange juice
1 tablespoon lemon juice
Confectioners' sugar
1/4 cup orange liqueur or brandy

Measure flour, the 2 tablespoons sugar, salt, eggs, egg yolks, milk, and the 2 tablespoons butter into a blender container or mixing bowl. Blend or beat with an electric or rotary beater until smooth.

Lightly grease a heavy 6-inch skillet and heat till a drop of water will dance on the surface. Remove from heat; pour 2 tablespoons batter into skillet. Tilt from side to side till the batter covers bottom evenly. Return skillet to heat and cook till underside is lightly browned, about 1 1/2 minutes. To remove invert skillet over paper toweling. Cook the remaining crepes in the same manner, greasing pan lightly each time. Keep warm till served.

Cream the 1/2 cup butter and 1/2 cup sugar; add peels and juices. Spread each crepe with about 1 tablespoon filling mixture. Roll up and sprinkle with confectioners' sugar. Arrange Crepes Suzette in chafing dish. Heat liqueur or brandy in small saucepan, ignite and pour over crepes. Makes 6 servings.

CRESCENT—A bun, roll, or cookie in the shape of a semicircle, tapering to points at each end. Crescent rolls are also referred to as butterhorns and croissants.

Crescents are most often rich in butter and may have a glaze. They are served as desserts, dinner breads, or sweet rolls at brunches. (See also *Croissant*.)

Spread warm crescent rolls with an orange glaze for a party bread to serve at brunch. Round out the menu with grilled ham and sausages, scrambled eggs, chilled fruit, and coffee.

To make crescents, roll dough into a 9-inch circle and cut into 12 wedges. Grasp each wedge at corners of the end opposite point. Begin rolling dough toward point.

While holding corners, flip point over the rolled dough. Place on a greased baking sheet with point down. Move ends of roll into a semicircle for a crescent shape.

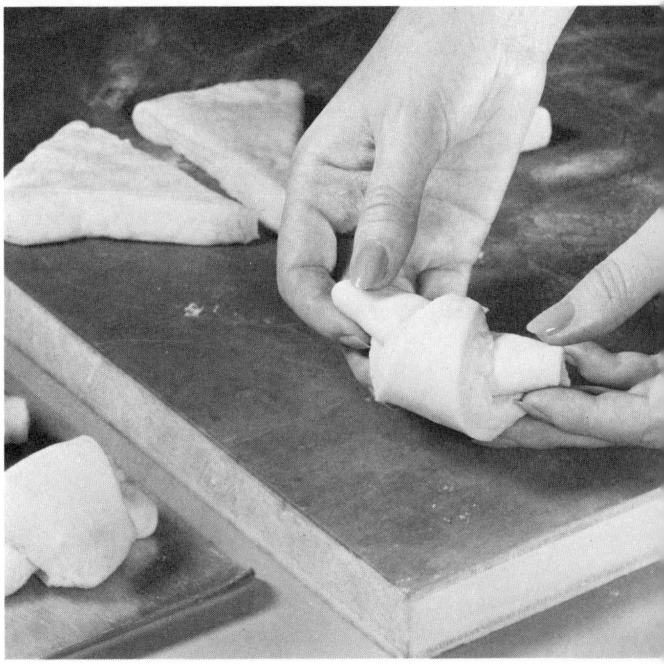

Orange Crescents

1 package active dry yeast
3 cups sifted all-purpose flour
1 cup milk
¼ cup sugar
¼ cup shortening
1 egg
1 teaspoon shredded orange peel
Orange Glaze

In large mixer bowl, combine yeast and 1¾ cups flour. Heat milk, sugar, shortening, and 1 teaspoon salt just till warm, stirring occasionally to melt shortening. Add to dry mixture in bowl; add egg and peel. Beat at low speed with electric mixer for ½ minute, scraping sides of bowl constantly. Beat 3 minutes at high speed. By hand, stir in remaining flour.

Place in greased bowl; turn to grease surface. Cover; refrigerate 2 hours. Divide in 2 parts. Roll each to 9-inch circle. Cut each in 12 wedges. Starting at wide end, roll up each wedge. Place points down, on greased baking sheets. Let rise in warm place till doubled, about 1¼ hours. Bake at 375° for 10 to 12 minutes. While warm, spread with glaze. Makes 24.

Orange Glaze: Combine 1½ cups sifted confectioners' sugar, ½ teaspoon grated orange peel, and dash salt. Add enough orange juice to make the desired consistency.

CRESS—Plants of the mustard family which have green, glossy, leaves. Some of the varieties are the garden cress or pepper cress, watercress, and Bell Isle cress.

Cress is desirable as a salad green and as a garnish. The pungent flavor accents soup, sandwich filling, and salad while adding color. Seven or eight sprigs of cress add only three calories, yet supply the A, B, and C vitamins.

CRIMP—1. To press food into folds or waves. 2. To gash the flesh of a fish.

Crimping in the first sense is usually associated with making pastry. An unbaked pastry shell is pressed into folds with fingers to make a decorative ridge.

Crimping by gashing the flesh of a fresh or freshly killed fish causes the muscles to contract, which makes the outer layer of the fish crisper when cooked.

CRINKLE—A shaped cookie that has a crackled top. (See also *Cookie*.)

Chocolate Crinkles

Cream ½ cup shortening, 1⅔ cups granulated sugar, and 2 teaspoons vanilla. Beat in 2 eggs, then two 1-ounce squares unsweetened chocolate, melted. Sift together 2 cups sifted all-purpose flour, 2 teaspoons baking powder, and ½ teaspoon salt; add alternately with ⅓ cup milk. Add ½ cup chopped walnuts.

Chill 3 hours. Form in 1-inch balls; roll in confectioners' sugar. Place on greased cookie sheet. Bake at 350° for 15 minutes. Makes 48.

CRISP—A term meaning brittle and firm. Crisping vegetables or crackers restores their firm texture. Vegetables are placed in cold water. Crackers are heated in the oven. Baked desserts with brittle, crumbly toppings are called crisps.

Lemon Crisp

Cream 6 tablespoons butter or margarine and ¾ cup brown sugar. Stir in 1 cup sifted all-purpose flour, ½ teaspoon baking soda, ½ teaspoon salt, ½ cup flaked coconut, and ¾ cup fine saltine cracker crumbs. Press *half* the mixture into an 8x8x2-inch baking pan. Bake at 350° for 10 minutes.

Meanwhile, combine ¾ cup granulated sugar, 2 tablespoons cornstarch, and ¼ teaspoon salt in a saucepan. Gradually stir in 1 cup hot water. Cook and stir till mixture is thickened and bubbly; boil about 2 minutes. Remove from heat. Stir small amount of hot mixture into 2 beaten egg yolks; return to hot mixture in saucepan. Bring to a boil, stirring constantly. Remove from heat. Gradually stir in ½ teaspoon grated lemon peel and ½ cup lemon juice.

Pour sauce over baked crust; top with reserved crumb mixture. Bake at 350° till brown, about 30 minutes. Cut into squares. Serve with whipped cream and twists of lemon. Serves 8.

CRISPER—A drawer or compartment in a refrigerator designed to keep fruits and vegetables at their best quality.

CRISSCROSS—A pattern formed by rows of lines crossing, as in a lattice pie top.

CROAKER—A small, saltwater fish caught in the waters off the Atlantic coast and the Gulf of Mexico. The name comes from the croaking sound made by the fish. The lean-fleshed fish averages about one pound in weight and is marketed whole or as fillets. (See also *Fish*.)

CROISSANT ***(krwä sän')***—Rich, flaky, French yeast rolls shaped like crescents. Croissant is the French word for crescent. The flaky texture is produced by rolling and rerolling the fresh dough, layered with chilled butter. Each layer separates slightly as the rolls bake, producing their characteristic light consistency. (See also *Roll*.)

Croissants

1½ cups butter
⅓ cup sifted all-purpose flour
• • •
2 packages active dry yeast
½ cup *warm* water
¾ cup milk, scalded
¼ cup sugar
1 teaspoon salt
1 beaten egg
3¾ to 4 cups sifted all-purpose flour
1 egg yolk
1 tablespoon milk

Cream butter with ⅓ cup flour. Roll mixture between waxed paper to 12x6-inches. Chill 1 hour or longer. Soften yeast in water. Combine milk, sugar, and salt. Cool to lukewarm. Add

Serve buttery-rich Croissants warm from the oven for flaky goodness. Accompany the puffy crescent-shaped rolls with your favorite jams, jellies, and decorative butter curls.

yeast and egg; mix well. Add 3¾ *cups* flour or enough to make soft dough. Knead on floured surface. Roll to 14-inch square. Place *chilled* butter on one half; fold over other half; seal edges. Roll to 20x12 inches; seal edges.

Fold in thirds so there are 3 layers. (If butter softens, chill after each rolling.) Roll to 20x12 inches again. Fold and roll twice more; seal edges. Fold in thirds to 12x7 inches. Chill 45 minutes. Cut dough crosswise in fourths. Roll each fourth (keep remainder chilled) to 22x7 inches, paper-thin. Cut in 10 pie-shaped wedges, 4 inches at base and 7 inches long. Put together the extra ½-wedges left at each end.

To shape rolls, begin with base (if dough has shrunk back, pull to original size) and roll loosely toward point. Place 3 inches apart on *ungreased* baking sheet, point down; curve ends. Cover; let double, 30 to 45 minutes. Beat egg yolk with milk; brush on rolls. Bake at 375° for 12 to 15 minutes. Makes 40.

CROOKNECK SQUASH—A kind of summer squash with a curved, swanlike neck. The nubby, warted skin is light yellow in young squash and deep yellow when mature. It grows to be eight to ten inches long and three inches thick. (See also *Squash.*)

Crookneck Curry, served in sauce dishes, combines crookneck squash with a curry mixture to become a vegetable delight.

Crookneck Curry

3 medium yellow crookneck squash
2 tablespoons butter or margarine, melted
¼ to ½ teaspoon curry powder

Cut squash crosswise into ¼-inch slices. Cook in small amount boiling salted water till tender; drain. Combine melted butter or margarine and curry powder with ¼ teaspoon salt and dash pepper. Drizzle over squash. Serves 6.

Confetti Squash

Steam tiny yellow squash (less than 3 inches long) till tender. Split lengthwise and brush with melted butter. Season. Sprinkle with snipped parsley and chopped canned pimiento. Place in shallow pan; heat in 350° oven.

CROQUETTE ***(krō ket')*** — Shaped balls, cones, or rolls of meat, poultry, or vegetables coated with a savory sauce, crumb coated, and deep fried. They have a crisp brown crust and a tender, moist interior.

Fat-fry small quantities of croquettes at one time to prevent temperature dropping. This assures a crisp, even, brown texture.

Drizzle packaged, frozen peas in cream sauce over crispy ham croquettes. Garnish with green parsley sprigs.

Ham and Rice Croquettes

1 10½-ounce can condensed cream of celery soup
1 pound ground cooked ham (3 cups)
1 cup cooked rice
1 tablespoon finely chopped onion
1 tablespoon finely chopped green pepper
1 to 2 tablespoons prepared mustard
1 beaten egg
1 cup fine bread crumbs
2 8-ounce packages frozen peas in cream sauce

Blend the first 6 ingredients thoroughly; chill. Shape mixture into croquettes, using about ¼ cup per croquette. Dip in egg, then in crumbs; let stand a few minutes. Fry 2 or 3 at a time in deep hot fat (365°) till brown, 3 to 5 minutes. Check temperature, making sure it remains at 365°. Drain croquettes on paper toweling. Prepare peas in cream sauce according to package directions; spoon sauce over croquettes before serving. Makes 8 to 10 servings.

Ham Croquettes

3 tablespoons butter
¼ cup all-purpose flour
¾ cup milk
2 cups coarsely ground cooked ham
1 teaspoon grated onion
Bread crumbs
2 teaspoons prepared mustard
1 beaten egg
Creamy Egg Sauce

Melt butter, blend in flour, and add milk all at once. Cook and stir till thick and bubbly; cook and stir 1 minute. Remove from heat. Add ham, onion, and mustard; blend well. Chill.

Shape mixture into 8 to 10 balls. Roll balls in bread crumbs and shape into cones, handling lightly. Combine egg with 2 tablespoons water. Dip into egg and water mixture; roll in crumbs again. Fry in deep hot fat (365°) till heated through, 1½ to 2 minutes. Drain. Serve with Creamy Egg Sauce. Makes 8 to 10 servings.

Creamy Egg Sauce: Melt 2 tablespoons butter; blend in 2 tablespoons flour, ¼ teaspoon salt, and dash white pepper. Add 1 cup milk. Cook and stir till mixture is thick and bubbly. Gently add 1 cup chopped hard-cooked egg.

CROUSTADE ***(krōō städ')***—A term used for a shell or container of toasted bread, shaped rice or pasta, or mashed potatoes. It may be baked or fried, then filled with various creamed meat, seafood, vegetable, or hors d'oeuvres mixtures.

Toast Cups

Trim crusts from 4 slices white bread. Spread bread with ¼ cup softened butter or margarine. Carefully press into *ungreased* medium muffin cups. Toast bread cups at 350° for about 15 minutes. Makes 4 toast cups.

CROUTE ***(krōōt)***—Toasted bread cases used for appetizer and dessert fillings.

CROUTON—A small piece of bread, usually diced, that has been oven toasted or browned in a buttered skillet. Croutons are used for garnishing soups, salads, and scrambled eggs; in bread puddings and stuffings; and as casserole toppings.

Serve croutons with bacon bits and shredded Cheddar cheese in small dishes as toppers for hot cooked beans and squash. Save any remaining croutons to add to a green tossed salad. Plan to prepare the croutons and the other toppers a day ahead. Cook six to eight extra slices of bacon at breakfast time. Buy the convenient packaged shredded Cheddar cheese to save preparation time.

Packaged croutons, either plain or seasoned, are available in supermarkets. The seasoned croutons may be flavored with garlic, cheese, or herbs. Heat packaged croutons on a baking sheet in a moderate oven to crisp them before serving.

Garlic Croutons

Vegetables, salads, and main dishes become special courses when topped with toasted garlic cubes—

4 to 5 slices bread
3 tablespoons butter or margarine
½ teaspoon garlic salt

To make croutons, cut 4 to 5 slices of bread into cubes to measure 3 cups. Melt butter or margarine in oven-proof skillet stirring in garlic salt. Drop bread cubes in mixture and toss to coat. Toast in a 225° oven till croutons are quite dry and crispy, about 2 hours. Use as a topper for salads, casseroles, or vegetables, or store in refrigerator and reheat them in the oven on a baking sheet when needed.

Toasted Croutons

Try asparagus, green beans, broccoli, and cauliflower with these crunchy croutons—

Dice white, whole wheat, or rye bread in tiny squares (about ⅛ inch). Brown the bread squares in a little butter in a skillet or the oven, or fry in deep hot fat. Season with salt and pepper, curry powder, or any favorite herb. Serve crispy croutons with cooked vegetables for a zesty flavor and delightful texture or toss atop a big green salad.

Drop diced bread cubes in melted butter or margarine with added seasonings and toss to coat. Heat in oven till dry and crisp.

CROWN ROAST—A roast shaped like a crown and made by sewing rib sections of lamb, pork, or veal in a circle. The ends of the ribs are "Frenched"; that is, a uniform amount of meat (usually one inch) is removed from each rib end.

A crown roast usually will have to be ordered several days in advance. When buying, ask the meatman to tie up the crown, scrape the rib ends, and grind up the scraped meat for the stuffing.

To prepare crown roast, attach aluminum foil to the bone ends to prevent scorching while roasting. Before the end of roasting time, fill the crown center with an herb-seasoned stuffing and roast till done. Unstuffed crown roasts need only be inverted with bones down to form a rack during roasting. Hot vegetables or fruit mixtures can be added to the center of the crown roast before serving.

To carve the roast, insert carving fork firmly between ribs to steady roast and cut downward between the ribs allowing one or two ribs for each slice. Lift slice with knife blade using fork to hold it firm while transferring to plate. (See also *Roast.*)

Ginger-Glazed Crown Roast of Pork

Glossy ginger-glazed crown roast entices company appetites and invites lavish compliments—

1 4- to 5-pound crown roast of pork*

• • •

½ cup pineapple juice
1 tablespoon minced preserved or candied ginger
2 tablespoons light molasses

Place crown roast of pork in shallow roasting pan turning the bone ends down. Insert meat thermometer in loin part of roast, making sure the end of the thermometer does not rest on bone or in fat. Roast at 325° till meat thermometer registers 170°, about 2¼ to 2¾ hours. In small bowl combine pineapple juice, ginger, and light molasses; baste roast with ginger glaze 4 times during the last hour of roasting. Makes 8 to 10 servings.

*Have meatman tie roast securely around loin area as well as near bones. This keeps the tender meat together during roasting.

Turn rib bones down forming a rack if the crown roast is to be filled with potatoes or other hot vegetables after roasting.

Festive crown roast of pork

←Easy-to-carve Crown Roast of Pork filled with tasty stuffing and citrus garnish is pretty enough to set before a king.

Corn-Stuffed Crown Roast of Pork

Set a festive pork crown on the dinner table—

1 5½- to 6-pound crown roast of pork (14 to 16 ribs)
1 17-ounce can cream-style corn
1 12-ounce can vacuum-packed whole kernel corn, drained
1 beaten egg
1 cup soft bread crumbs
¼ cup chopped onion
¼ cup chopped green pepper
2 tablespoons chopped canned pimiento
1 teaspoon salt
Dash pepper

Have crown roast of pork made from strip of pork loin from which backbone has been removed. Have roast tied securely around loin area as well as near bones, and have meat "Frenched" by removing 1 inch meat from rib tips. Season roast. Place in shallow roasting pan, bone ends up; wrap tips in aluminum foil to avoid charring. Insert meat thermometer in loin, making sure it does not rest on bone or in fat. Roast, uncovered, at 325° till thermometer reads 170°, about 2½ to 3 hours.

To make stuffing, measure and mix remaining ingredients together in a large bowl. An hour before meat is done, fill crown center with Corn Stuffing. Place remaining stuffing in casserole. Dot with butter; bake alongside crown roast at 325°. Garnish with green parsley or citrus fruit. Cut between each roast rib for custom-sized servings. Cut and serve Corn Stuffing along with crown roast of pork.

CRULLER—A twisted or oval-shaped sweet cake made of rolled dough and fat, then deep fried. A sister to the doughnut, the name cruller comes from the Dutch word *krulle,* meaning "twisted cake." Shapes are made by rolling out the dough, cutting it into strips, doubling the strips, and twisting to shape. Braids can be made by twisting two pieces together with ends pinched together. Crullers fried in deep fat swell into golden puffy cakes. Granulated or powdered sugar is sprinkled on the cooked cake as a final step to making sweet crullers. (See also *Doughnut.*)

For chocolate-coated candy crumbs, place candies in a plastic bag on a cutting board. Pound with the flat end of a mallet.

Cookie or cracker crumbs are made by crushing the whole cookies with a rolling pin. A blender also makes fine, even crumbs.

CRUMB—1. To coat or bread a food usually with bread, cereal, or cracker crumbs. 2. To crush, roll, or grind a food into fine pieces. 3. A small particle of any food that breaks easily into pieces.

There are numerous ways in which crumbs of one kind or another are used in cooking. Crumbs made from bread or plain crackers may be used to thicken or bind ingredients or to coat foods that are to be baked or fried. Similar crumbs, buttered, top casseroles. Crumbs made from graham crackers, vanilla wafers, gingersnaps, or zwieback make tasty pie shells.

Make your own crumbs, as suggested here, or look for convenience items such as packaged bread, cornflake, and graham cracker crumbs in the supermarket.

Bread Crumbs

Tear slices of fresh bread into quarters. Using small amounts at a time, add to blender. Turn blender on and off quickly till desired fineness results. About 1 slice bread (depending on thickness) makes 1 cup soft bread crumbs.

For fine dry bread crumbs, dry bread in oven. Crush with rolling pin till fine, or break up in large pieces and add to blender container, a small amount at a time. Blend quickly till desired fineness results. Four slices bread (depending on thickness) makes 1 cup crumbs.

Buttery Bread Crumbs

Combine ½ cup fine dry bread crumbs with 2 tablespoons butter or margarine, melted. Sprinkle top of casserole with mixture. Makes enough to trim a 1-quart casserole or four 8-ounce individual baking dishes.

CRUMB CRUST—A crust for an appetizer, entrée, side dish, or dessert recipe made by pressing a buttered crumb mixture into a pan, usually a pie plate. Whether the crumb crust is baked or not depends on the type of mixture used and, often, personal taste. Baking produces a more compact crust that does not shatter easily. (See *Crust, Pastry* for additional information.)

Vanilla Wafer Crust

1½ cups fine vanilla wafer crumbs (36 wafers)
6 tablespoons butter or margarine, melted

Mix together crumbs and butter. Press firmly into a 9-inch pie plate. Chill till set.

Graham Cracker Crust

1¼ cups fine graham cracker crumbs
¼ cup sugar
6 tablespoons butter or margarine, melted

Combine graham cracker crumbs, sugar, and butter; mix. Press firmly into a 9-inch pie plate. Bake at 375° till edges are browned, about 6 to 8 minutes; cool. If unbaked crust is desired, chill 45 minutes; fill.

To shape an even crumb crust, spoon crumbs in bottom of a 9-inch pie plate. With an 8-inch pie plate, press into crumb mixture.

Loosen a crumb crust by wrapping a hot wet towel around bottom and sides of plate. Hold against plate a few minutes.

Rather moist, compact foods such as blue cheese are most easily crumbled with a fork. Dry foods can be crumbled by hand.

Chocolate-Wafer Crust

Combine 1½ cups fine chocolate-wafer crumbs and 6 tablespoons butter or margarine, melted. Press firmly into 9-inch pie plate. Chill till set.

CRUMBLE—1. A dessert, such as a fruit crisp, topped with a crumbly mixture of flour, shortening, and sugar. The topping bakes to a crisp texture. 2. To break a food into small irregular-sized pieces.

CRUMPET—A soft-textured, unsweetened, English tea or breakfast bread. Once a home-baked delight, now crumpets are produced commercially. The batter, composed of flour, milk, butter, egg, salt, and yeast, is poured into metal rings and baked on a griddle rather than in the oven.

The baked crumpets are split and toasted before being served. Butter and jam are standard accompaniments. Although similar to English muffins, crumpets are softer in texture and are identified by large surface holes that develop during baking. (See also *English Cookery*.)

CRUSH—To apply pressure to food pieces by pounding or grinding so as to break down structure, soften the food, and/or release juices or aroma. For example, fruits are crushed to extract juice for jelly making. Dried bread or crisp cookies are crushed with a rolling pin when a recipe specifies crumbs as a coating or topping for a soft food or mixture. Dried herbs are crushed before using to release flavor.

CRUST—1. The crisp, browned exterior of a baked, sautéed, roasted, or fried food. 2. The baked pastry shell or crumb mixture that lines a pie pan and holds the filling, or the pastry cover for a pie or cobbler. 3. The dough or pastry used to encase small amounts of filling for turnovers or to wrap around large pieces of meat such as baked ham or beef tenderloin. 4. The undesirable drying out of the surface of foods that have not been wrapped or stored properly in the refrigerator or freezer.

When making pies or cobblers, choose a crust from the wide variety available. Besides pastry or biscuit dough crusts, there are chocolate, gingersnap, cereal, coconut, and many others. Some are baked and others are chilled in the refrigerator. The Coconut Crust is an example of a crust which is browned in the oven. The Cornflake Crust will set up when chilled well in the refrigerator. Baking is not necessary.

Coconut Crust

Fill with creamy vanilla or chocolate pudding—

Combine one 3½-ounce can flaked coconut (1⅓ cups) and 2 tablespoons butter or margarine, melted. Press around the bottom and sides of a 9-inch pie plate. Bake at 325° till coconut is light golden brown, about 15 minutes.

Cornflake Crust

Scoop ice cream generously into the shell, then pass a favorite sundae topping—

Combine 1 cup crushed cornflakes *or* crisp rice cereal, with ¼ cup sugar and ⅓ cup butter, melted. Press in 9-inch pie plate. Chill.

Crusts for wrapping meats are generally of two types. In one, the mixture is designed only to hold in the juices during baking. The crust is peeled off and discarded before serving. However, when the dish being prepared is as glamorous as Beef Wellington, the crust, made of puff pastry, is the crowning touch which adds elegance to the final dish. (See *Crumb Crust, Pastry* for additional information.)

CRUSTACEAN—Any of a large class of marine and freshwater animals having crustlike shells. Included are lobsters, shrimp, and crabs. (See also *Shellfish.*)

CRYSTALLIZE—The action by which syrups and jams "sugar" or form crystals as they cool or dry out. Controlling the size and number of crystals is an important factor in successful candy making, particularly when making fudge or fondant varieties. Crystallized ginger and candied orange peel are examples of foods preserved by allowing sugar crystals to coat the outside surface of the food.

CUBA LIBRE—A beverage made of cola and rum, served in a tall glass over ice. It is usually flavored or garnished with fresh lime. (See also *Cocktail.*)

CUBE—To cut solid food into pieces with six equal square sides that are usually larger than one-fourth inch.

CUBE STEAK, MINUTE STEAK—A boneless cut of beef, usually from the round or sirloin tip, which has been tenderized by a machine that breaks up connective tissue in the meat. The machine was originally called a cubing machine; hence, the name of the steak. Today, however, the steak is more frequently marketed as Minute Steak. (See *Beef, Minute Steak* for additional information.)

CUCUMBER—The crisp, green-rinded fruit of a trailing vine belonging to the squash and gourd family. It is also a kin to many melons. Climbing and spreading readily, the stem is stiff and hairy with coil-like tendrils that can be trained to climb. The deep golden flowers measure an inch or

When cubing foods, use a sharp knife to make lengthwise cuts of the desired width. Similar crosswise cuts finish the task.

more across. Although the young fruit is rather prickly, the mature fruit, especially among the hybrid varieties, is smooth.

The cucumber is believed to be native to India, where it has been grown for more than 3,000 years. Early writings indicate the cucumber was served in ancient China and it is mentioned in the Old Testament as a food eaten in Egypt. The Romans devised some hothouse varieties so the fruit could be served daily in the imperial household.

For centuries cucumbers have been served both fresh and pickled. In addition, numerous cosmetic properties have been attributed to the cucumber, and today there are still commercially made skin creams with cucumber as an ingredient.

Nutritional value: Cucumbers are low in calories; thus, they are prized in weight-watching diets. Half a medium cucumber has only seven calories. Because of their high water content, cucumbers are not particularly high in total food value.

Types of cucumbers: Final use, that is whether the "cuke" is to be sliced and served fresh or pickled in a brine, has been the guideline for horticulturists developing the cucumber varieties marketed today. Generally, those suitable for slicing and table use are six to nine inches in length with a dark to very dark green, smooth outer rind. However, for pickling purposes, both commercially and at home, cucumbers from one to three inches in length are the size preferred.

The gherkin, a small cucumber variety native to the West Indies, is always mentioned in a discussion of pickle making. Over the years it has been prized for its use in pickles. However, since small cucumbers of newer hybrid varieties can be mechanically harvested to better advantage, commercial pickle packers depend more upon hybrids than on the gherkin. Homemakers generally make pickles from special pickling cucumber varieties available for planting in the garden.

How to select: Cucumbers, whatever their intended use, should be fresh, firm, bright, and well shaped. Pass up those that look withered or shriveled as they are usually tough, rubbery, and somewhat bitter. Avoid, too, those that have an overgrown, puffy appearance and yellowing rind. Select pickling cucumbers according to the size desired for the type of whole or sliced pickle that is to be made.

How to store: Cucumbers should be washed, dried, and stored in the refrigerator where they will keep satisfactorily for one to two weeks. The edible wax with which cucumbers in the supermarket are sometimes coated to prevent wilting is tasteless. This wax may be scrubbed off or not, depending on your personal preference. However, do not peel cucumbers until just before they are used.

Because of their high water content, cucumbers do not freeze satisfactorily either by themselves or as an ingredient. This is a good thing to keep in mind when making frozen vegetable salads.

Sliced or cooked cucumbers may wilt or become soggy. One to two days in the refrigerator is maximum storage time.

How to prepare: The entire cucumber is edible and certainly looks attractive when sliced crosswise end to end for use on a relish tray or in a refreshing tossed or molded salad. It is no wonder that the phrase "cool as a cucumber" pays compliment to the person who looks fresh and unwilted on a very hot day.

Many people do not think of serving cucumbers as a cooked vegetable. Yet, as members of the squash family, they can be cut up and cooked till tender in boiling salted water. Halved cucumbers with the seeds scooped out may be brushed with butter and baked or stuffed in much the same way as acorn or zucchini squash for a menu change. Butter, salt, and pepper are the simplest of seasoners. A light sprinkle of herbs or a delicate cream sauce goes well with this mild-flavored vegetable, too. (See *Pickle, Salad, Vegetable* for additional information.)

Cucumber tips

- Personal choice or recipe requirements determine whether cucumbers are peeled or not.
- Run tines of fork lengthwise along a cucumber before slicing for frilled edges.
- For crisp slices, put cucumber slices in ice water, or vinegar or sour cream dressing immediately after cutting.

Sour Cream Cucumbers

Thinly slice 1 cucumber; sprinkle with 1 teaspoon salt; let stand 30 minutes. Drain.

Combine ½ cup dairy sour cream, 4 teaspoons vinegar, 1 to 2 drops bottled hot pepper sauce, 2 tablespoons snipped chives, ½ teaspoon dried dillweed, and dash pepper; pour over cucumbers. Chill. Makes 4 or 5 servings.

Salad in a circle

←A built-in garnish of cucumber slices trims this Cucumber Ring Supreme. Cherry tomatoes piled in the center add a bright note.

Vegetable Medley

2 cups chopped cucumbers
1 cup sliced radishes
1 cup sliced green onions
½ cup dairy sour cream
1 tablespoon lemon juice
½ teaspoon salt
⅛ teaspoon dry mustard

Combine vegetables. Blend sour cream, lemon juice, salt, and dry mustard; toss lightly with vegetable mixture. Chill. Serves 4 to 6.

Cucumber Ring Supreme

Cucumber-trim Layer
1 envelope unflavored gelatin (1 tablespoon)
2 tablespoons sugar
¾ teaspoon salt
⅔ cup water
2 tablespoons lemon juice
1 8-ounce package cream cheese, cubed and softened

• • •

About 6 medium peeled cucumbers
1 cup mayonnaise or salad dressing
3 tablespoons finely chopped onion
¼ cup snipped parsley

Prepare *Cucumber-trim Layer:* Mix ½ envelope (1½ teaspoons) unflavored gelatin, 1 tablespoon sugar, and ½ teaspoon salt in small saucepan. Add ¾ cup water; heat and stir till gelatin and sugar are dissolved. Stir in 2 tablespoons lemon juice. Pour into 6½-cup ring mold. Chill till partially set. Overlay thin slices from ½ unpeeled cucumber in bottom of mold. Chill till *almost* firm.

Meanwhile, mix the 1 envelope unflavored gelatin, sugar, and salt in small saucepan. Add water; stir mixture over low heat until gelatin and sugar are dissolved. Stir in lemon juice. Gradually beat hot gelatin mixture into softened cream cheese with a rotary beater blending till mixture is smooth.

Halve cucumbers and scrape out seeds; grind using fine blade, or finely shred. Measure 2 cups drained ground cucumber and add with remaining ingredients to cream cheese mixture. Pour over almost firm gelatin in mold. Chill salad in refrigerator till firm. Makes 8 servings.

Ham-Chicken Supreme

6 cups torn lettuce
1 cup diced cucumber
1 medium green pepper, cut in narrow strips
1 cup fully-cooked ham, cut in strips
1 cup cooked chicken, cut in strips
3 hard-cooked eggs, sliced
2 medium tomatoes, cut in wedges
½ cup salad oil
3 tablespoons vinegar
1 tablespoon prepared horseradish
½ teaspoon Worcestershire sauce
2 drops bottled hot pepper sauce
½ teaspoon salt
⅛ teaspoon pepper

Line individual salad bowls with lettuce. Arrange cucumber, green pepper, ham, chicken, eggs, and tomatoes in each. In screw-top jar, combine remaining ingredients for dressing. Cover and shake well. Pass dressing with salads. Makes 8 to 10 servings.

Chilled soups like Buttermilk-Cuke Soup look their "coolest" topped with crisp cucumber slices. (See *Buttermilk* for recipe.)

Cucumber Burgers

Unusual? Yes, but unusually good to eat—

1 medium unpeeled cucumber
½ cup dairy sour cream
¼ cup chopped onion
1 teaspoon salt
1 teaspoon lemon juice
Dash pepper
1½ pounds ground beef
6 hamburger buns, split

Shred enough unpeeled cucumber to measure ½ cup; drain thoroughly. Stir in sour cream, chopped onion, salt, lemon juice, and pepper. Add ground beef; mix well. Chill. Shape into 6 patties, ¾ inch thick. Broil 3 inches from heat 6 minutes. Turn; broil 4 minutes. Serve in hamburger buns. Makes 6 servings.

Blender Cucumber Salad

How easy it is to let an appliance do all the work for both salad and dressing—

1 large cucumber, peeled
1 3-ounce package lemon-flavored gelatin
1¼ cups boiling water

• • •

1 8-ounce carton cream-style cottage cheese
2 tablespoons sugar
4 teaspoons lemon juice
2 tablespoons milk
Lettuce

Slice cucumber into blender container. Cover and blend on high speed till puréed. Stop blender as needed to push cucumber down from sides. Measure cucumber; add water, if necessary, to make 1 cup.

Dissolve gelatin in boiling water; stir in cucumber. Chill gelatin mixture till partially set, stirring occasionally. Pour into 3½-cup ring mold. Chill till firm.

In blender container combine cottage cheese, sugar, and lemon juice; blend till creamy. Add milk, one tablespoon at a time, till dressing is of the desired consistency.

Unmold salad onto lettuce-lined platter. Pass cottage cheese dressing. Serves 4 to 6.

Cucumber Basket

Hollow out a 3-inch length of unpeeled cucumber, leaving 1/4-inch base and walls. Mark lengthwise strips around outside. Cut rind down every other strip of peel, *almost* to base. Crisp in ice water; drain. Cut strips of peel from remaining cucumber. Shape in circles; secure with wooden picks at base of basket. Fill with mayonnaise or salad dressing. Trim with parsley or paprika. Serve with tossed or molded salads. Another time, fill cucumber basket with tartar or seafood-cocktail sauce and pass with fish or shellfish.

Fresh Cucumber Relish

Perky dill-flavored accompaniment to pass with platter of sliced tomatoes or cold meats—

3 medium cucumbers
1/2 medium onion
• • •
1/3 cup vinegar
1 tablespoon sugar
1/2 teaspoon salt
1/4 teaspoon dried dillweed

Slice cucumbers in half lengthwise; scoop out seeds and discard. With food chopper, using coarse blade, grind cucumbers and onion; drain. Stir in remaining ingredients. Chill thoroughly. Makes about 1 3/4 cups.

Cucumber Sauce

So good with fish and seafood—

1 medium, unpeeled cucumber
1/2 cup dairy sour cream
1/4 cup mayonnaise
1 tablespoon snipped parsley
2 teaspoons grated onion
2 teaspoons vinegar
1/4 teaspoon salt
Dash pepper

Cut cucumber in half lengthwise; scoop out seeds. Shred enough cucumber to make 1 cup; do not drain. Combine sour cream, mayonnaise, parsley, onion, vinegar, salt, and pepper. Blend well. Chill. Makes 1 1/2 cups.

Cucumber baskets begin with a hollowed-out chunk of cucumber. Careful marking and cutting of the rind adds decoration.

Cabbage-Cucumber Slaw

3 cups shredded cabbage
1 cup shredded red cabbage
1 cup halved slices unpeeled cucumber
1/2 cup chopped celery
2 tablespoons chopped onion
Salt
Pepper
• • •
2 tablespoons French salad dressing
2 tablespoons mayonnaise or salad dressing

Combine cabbage, cucumber slices, celery, and onion; chill. Season to taste with salt and pepper. At serving time, blend French salad dressing and mayonnaise; toss with cabbage mixture. Makes 8 servings.

CUMBERLAND SAUCE—A thickened sauce of English origin that is served with ham or game meats. Standard flavorings include currant jelly, red wine, orange peel and juice. Flavor is peaked by ginger, dry mustard, cayenne, or lemon juice.

Cumberland Sauce

Combine ½ teaspoon shredded orange peel, ¾ cup orange juice, ½ cup currant jelly, 2 tablespoons claret, and ¼ teaspoon ground ginger in saucepan. Heat till jelly melts, stirring occasionally. Blend 4 teaspoons cornstarch and 1 tablespoon lemon juice till smooth; stir into jelly mixture. Cook and stir till mixture is thick and bubbly; cook 1 to 2 minutes longer. Serve Cumberland Sauce hot or cold with ham or game meats. Makes about 1½ cups.

CUMIN ***(kum' uhn)***—An herb related to parsley and a close cousin to caraway. Like some other herbs and spices, cumin has a Mediterranean origin, but its popularity in food has spread throughout the world.

Historical records provide interesting facts on past superstitions concerning the uses of cumin. One of these symbolized cumin as a miser. Another advised a bride and groom to carry cumin during the wedding ceremony to assure themselves a happy life together. Farmers who cursed cumin seed while sowing their crops supposedly were rewarded with a bountiful harvest.

In reality, cumin was used as a drug ingredient in Babylonia and Assyria. Biblical writings list cumin as a tithing spice. In addition, the Greeks and Romans used cumin as a food preservative.

Today, the aromatic seed of the cumin plant, either whole or ground, is the portion used for commercial and home cooking purposes. Although cumin is grown throughout the Mediterranean region, the United States imports are mainly from Iran, Morocco, Lebanon, and Syria.

Cumin's flavor has been described as being strong, warm, and slightly bitter, yet nutty. By itself or as an ingredient in curry powder or chili powder, cumin spices a variety of international foods and beverages, such as Indian curries, hot Mexican dishes, a German liqueur called Kümmel, Arabian salads, and Dutch or Swiss cheeses called Kumminost.

Because of its concentrated flavor, cumin should be added to foods sparingly. It is an excellent appetite stimulant when used in appetizers. It is also recommended for use in soups, sauces, salad dressings, and cookies and with foods such as cheese, egg, cabbage, fish, ground beef, potato, and game. (See also *Herb*.)

Cumin Burgers

Combine 1 pound ground beef, 2 teaspoons instant minced onion, ½ teaspoon salt, ¼ teaspoon ground cumin seed, dash garlic powder, and dash pepper. Shape into 4 patties, ¾ inch thick. Grill over *medium* coals for 6 minutes. Turn and grill 4 to 6 minutes more. Place in 4 buns, split and toasted. Serves 4.

Sour Cream Baked Potatoes

4 medium baking potatoes
1 envelope sour cream sauce mix
¾ cup milk
½ teaspoon ground cumin seed
2 tablespoons butter or margarine
Paprika

Scrub potatoes; prick with fork. Bake at 425° for 50 to 60 minutes. Blend together sauce mix, milk, ½ teaspoon salt, cumin, and dash pepper; set aside for 10 minutes. Cut thin slice from top of each potato; discard. Scoop out center of potatoes; add to sour cream mixture. Stir in butter or margarine.

Beat potato mixture till fluffy, adding more milk, if necessary. Spoon mixture back into potato shells. Sprinkle with paprika. Bake at 375° for 20 to 25 minutes. Top with crisp-cooked bacon curls, if desired. Makes 4 servings.

CUP—A small, open vessel with attached handle intended primarily to hold liquids. In the United States, the cup has become a common measuring unit. One standard cup, as determined by the National Bureau of Standards, contains 8 fluid ounces, 16 tablespoons, or ½ pint.